PEEL'S
ENGLAND

Other books by J. H. B. Peel include:

Poetry
Light And Shade

Essays
Country Talk
More Country Talk
New Country Talk
Country Talk Again

Travel
Portrait of the Thames
Portrait of the Severn
Portrait of Exmoor
An Englishman's Home
Along the Pennine Way
Along the Roman Roads of Britain
Along the Green Roads of Britain

PEEL'S ENGLAND

J H B Peel

With Photographs by Kenneth Scowen

David & Charles
Newton Abbot London North Pomfret (Vt) Vancouver

Lords and Commons of England, consider what Nation it is whereof ye are.

John Milton

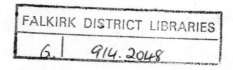

ISBN 0 7153 7380 3

Set in 11pt. on 13pt. Baskerville by G. C. Typeset Limited, Bolton
and printed in Great Britain
by Redwood Burn Limited, Trowbridge and Esher
for David & Charles (Publishers) Limited
Brunel House, Newton Abbot, Devon

Published in the United States of America
by David & Charles Inc
North Pomfret, Vermont 05053, USA

Published in Canada
by Douglas David & Charles Limited
1875 Welch Street, North Vancouver, BC

CONTENTS

1 A TRAIN OF THOUGHT   7

2 THE SOUTH EAST   11

3 THE SOUTH MIDLANDS   36

4 EAST ANGLIA   64

5 THE NORTH EAST   90

6 THE BORDER COUNTRY   103

7 LAKELAND   127

8 THE MARCHES   140

9 THE SOUTH WEST   166

   INDEX   190

1 A TRAIN OF THOUGHT

The train carrying me westward spanned the shires and the centuries of England. Some of the sights — a mountain or a river — lingered long enough for the mind to parse them; others — a cottage or a cyclist — departed on arrival, straining the eye from its socket. Yet amid that evanescence one thing remained constant, the Englishry, whose woof and warp wove a tapestry both timeless and topical: an old man, for instance, scything the perimeter of an airfield . . . cattle stockstill as toys in a child's farmyard . . . silted canals looping the loop like an endless lilypond . . . housewives pegging petticoats on a Monday morning breeze . . . snowposts pointing winterward . . . love's labour found in a whiff of wallflowers windowboxing a back street bedroom . . . a cathedral surmounting the dead sea of Mammon's jetsam . . . a Tudor manor house, occupied by descendants of the squire who built it.

Those sights, of course, are common. I had seen them many times, and always with the anticipation of journeys yet to come. On this journey, however, the sights caused me to look back, by reminding me that I had spent more than half a century exploring Britain in general and England in particular. Would it not seem fitting, therefore, to share my travels, not only with Englishfolk but also with the men and women of other nations, who, because they love their own land, are able to extend that courtesy throughout the world, knowing that love is founded on old acquaintance, critical insight, reasonable tolerance.

So, the passing sights symbolised the passing years; and from them grew this book, not without difficulty. Consider, for example, the problem of size. Now although England looks small on the map, it becomes very large indeed when compressed between the covers of a book. Some writers have tried to cut their losses by increasing their wordage. Among them was Daniel Defoe, who squeezed the kingdom into two volumes which he named *A Tour through the Whole of Great Britain*. He further reduced his handicap by narrowing the range: 'Antiquity,' he declared, 'is not my search in this work'. Defoe preferred to report such matters as the price of mutton at Manchester in 1724 and the tonnage of wool at Cirencester in 1725. Even so, he found it impossible to banish 'antiquity' from his pages. In Caithness he visited John o'Groat's House; in Northumberland he saw Hadrian's Wall; in Wiltshire he measured Stonehenge. As a result, he produced not only a commercial treatise but also a travelogue that is read by people who feel no great interest in wool, and are total abstainers from mutton.

Defoe was a townsman. I on the other hand, am a countryman. Of large cities and industrial regions I know very little, chiefly because I find it difficult to breathe there, and more than difficult to endure the sound of progress. My life is passed in deep country, far from motorways and factories. Such profound rustication may at first sight seem an impediment, and would indeed have proved so, had I attempted to analyse the cotton trade or the entertainment industry. But in this book I have been concerned rather with everything in general than with anything in particular, so that an encounter with a wheelwright (the last of his kind in his county) is followed by a visit to a derelict church, which in turn gives way to haymaking, battleships, place-names, Latin poetry, fishermen, smugglers, Julius Caesar, William Caxton, Oliver Cromwell, Horatio Nelson, Sarah Siddons, Thomas Gray, Dorothy Wordsworth, Lloyd George, Mary Webb, Rudyard Kipling; interspersed with signposts, mountains, cooking, cattle, life, death, income tax, blackbirds, bison, geology, dialect; together with one or two other topics, such, for example, as the origins or genealogy of the English, and the derivation of their name, and the multiplicity of reasons why they won and so swiftly lost the world's largest empire.

You may marvel that any journey ever could be planned to encompass so many and such diverse topics. The explanation is simple; the journey was *not* planned to encompass them; they happened to lie en route or within a few miles of it. What, then, *is* the route? It is some of the roads, rivers, paths, coasts, and tracks which I have traversed since the year 1913. The route, however, does not enter every English county. If it did, the results would resemble the view from an aircraft . . . superficial because supersonic. Instead, the route begins at Dover, enters Sussex, avoids London and then veers north-west to the Southern Midlands, whose classic places are Oxford and Stratford-upon-Avon. Bearing east, we reach Cambridge, the Fens, and the Norfolk coast. Now follows a long haul to Lincolnshire, Yorkshire, Durham and Northumberland, whence we head south through Lakeland, Cheshire, and the Welsh Marches. From Tintern Abbey we cross the River Severn, westward-bound for Coleridge's Quantocks, Jan Ridd's Exmoor, and Hawker's Atlantic coast. Finally, having avoided the summer car queues, we climb the roof of Cornwall, sail the coast of Roseland and come at last to Land's End.

On a map the route appears simple, but it did not always go according to plan. Sometimes I found myself adrift in a strange place; at other times I played truant. Yet all was for the best because the detours added new delight to perennial wonder. Moreover, the re-travelling of earlier journeys brought the scene up-to-date. It revealed the changes. It confirmed the constancy. It invited me to amble where formerly I had hurried. It warned me to skip the *longueurs*.

During the journey, I encountered many aspects of the tourist trade, a controversial subject. If, for example, you rejoice that Cornwall has become a commercialised playground, then my remarks about tourism will seem offensive, and you will probably reject them as 'snobbish' or 'unrealistic'. If, on the other hand, you rejoice that Leicestershire has *not* become a commercialised playground, then my remarks on tourism will seem inoffensive, and you will probably accept them as 'public-spirited' or 'realistic'. Though I value approval in this matter, I do not fear disapproval. Nor shall I apologise for flouting the convention which now requires an Englishman to speak of litres instead of pints, of metres instead of yards, of Cumbria instead of Westmorland. For a thousand years the men of this kingdom have measured their land in acres, their hosiery in inches, their timber in tons; and although I welcome every worthy visitor from other lands, I will not alienate the legacy of this land in order to please a common marketplace.

There remains a postscript, and it concerns patriotism or love of one's country. National arrogance is not love; it is infatuation, an immature and self-centred excess, which remains blind not only to the defects of its own country but also to the merits of other countries. True love, by contrast, is wide-eyed. It perceives goodness and badness wherever they appear. It achieves a degree of objectivity and justice. It is a kind of Esperanto, a universal language of the heart. The more, therefore, you do love England, the more you love Russia and Scotland and Spain, for they, too, possess an inimitable temperament, an indigenous language, a unique history. People who deride patriotism are like birds that foul their own nest, or claim to be fledglings of the world, as much at home in Iceland as in Zanzibar. Shakespeare scorned the Englishman who slanders England. Such a renegade, he said, is forever belittling 'all the benefits of his own country, out of love with his own nativity'. But Shakespeare did not leave it at that. He went further. He composed England's greatest love song:

This happy breed of men, this little world,
This precious stone, set in the silver sea . . .

Many of Shakespeare's audience were 'groundlings' who seldom washed and sometimes went hungry. He would never have written that love song if it had been likely to evoke a shower of rotten eggs. What was good enough for Shakespeare would not now seem good enough for us who enjoy a comfort and security which no Elizabethan could have imagined. How much greater, therefore, is our own debt to the men and women who created, nurtured, and continue to sustain

This blessed plot, this earth, this realm, this England.

2 THE SOUTH EAST

Medieval Dover was called 'The Key of England'. If an invader could capture that key he might conquer the entire kingdom, using the harbour as a supply base, the castle as a springboard, and the Roman Watling Street as a highway. Dover, in short, is what the Romans would have called *locus classicus* or a famous example, for it was here, or somewhere close by, that our history began to be written by a Roman general, Gaius Julius, who made notes for despatches about his campaigns in Britain and Gaul. Yet Dover is something more than a key or military chessman. It is a nursery of the English nation. If you wish to discover the genesis of that nation you must go back nearly ten thousand years, to a time when Britain was joined with the continent of Europe, scarcely a day's march for the savages who shambled overland from Calais. Those ancestors, however, are so remote that they make the Bronze Age Celts seem relatively modern. A Victorian scholar, Sir John Rhys, believed that the Celts reached Europe from the East during the Iron Age, thereafter dividing into three parts — Gaulish, Cymric, Goildelic — representing France, Wales, and Ireland (whence the Goildelic Celts migrated to Scotland). Modern historians take a more cautious view. Dr Anne Ross, for instance, has suggested that the word 'Celt' connotes no more than certain racial and linguistic attributes of a people who reached Europe about the year 1300 BC. The British Celts, at all events, either merged with or were driven westward by Romans, Saxons, Jutes, Angles, Vikings, Normans; all of whom contributed to the making of the English nation; and one of whom bequeathed their own name, Angles or *Engle*, so that *Engle-land* became England.

Dover itself looks well from the sea. The white cliffs abide, but not a great deal else that Dorothy Wordsworth would now recognise. Even in 1802 she noticed 'a very old Building . . . which had a strange effect among so many new ones that are springing up everywhere'. Modern visitors to Dover must seek out the jewels from a pastework of Victorian and Atomic addenda; notably a Roman bathhouse, a medieval cloth hall, the smallest round church in Britain (built by the Knights Templars), and on the clifftop a trio of castle and lighthouse and church. When Celia Fiennes arrived, in 1697, she reported that the castle was 'left much in decay and ruinated, only a small appartment for the Governour of three or four roomes, else the whole is spoyl'd . . .'. Miss Fiennes felt a personal interest because she was a granddaughter of Lord Saye and Sele, whose ancestors had been hereditary Constables of Dover Castle for one hundred-and-fifty years. During the thirteenth century the constable acquired wider powers and with them another title, Lord Warden of the Cinque Ports, a defensive and commercial confederation, which ultimately co-opted thirty-two harbours and fishing villages on the Channel coast. The wardens made their official residence in Walmer Castle at Deal; the greatest among them being Sir Winston Spencer-Churchill. Built partly of rubble from the Roman town, Dover Castle is perhaps the most impressive in Britain, being older than Windsor, larger than Carisbrooke, loftier than Bamburgh.

Within a stone's throw of the castle, nearly five hundred feet above the sea, stands the Saxon church of St Mary-in-Castro (that is, within the *castra* or 'Roman camp'). Alongside the church stands a pharos or Roman lighthouse, whose upper parts are medieval, while the lower section, forty feet high, is of flint and Roman brick. This ancient monument symbolises the earliest aspects of *Romanitas*, the Roman legacy. Dover's Roman name was *Dubrae*, a Latin version of the Celtic *dubra* or 'river', nowadays called the River Dour. When the Legions occupied Britain in AD 43 they saw *Dubrae* as the key not only to their new territory but also to Rome itself; and from Dover they built the first of their major British roads, Watling Street, which led to London, and was soon afterwards extended to the Welsh Marches.

Dover excels even the Tower of London as a spectator of historic comings and goings. It saw Henry V returning from

Agincourt with his band of brothers 'that fought with us upon Saint Crispin's day'. It saw the Tudor seadogs (out-gunned and out-numbered) chasing the Armada into the North Sea and thence to destruction. It saw England (once more short of men and ships) awaiting the fleet wherewith Bonaparte planned to invade her. It saw the sailors of the 1914 Dover Patrol (again ill-equipped) who, as Joseph Conrad recalled, 'made a sacrifice of their lives every time they went out for a turn of duty'. It saw a British Expeditionary Force (yet again out-gunned and out-numbered) being rescued from the Dunkirk beaches.. It saw, a few years later, the greatest naval invasion ever launched or ever likely to be launched. Medieval crusaders, Tudor cardinals, Stuart kings, Hanoverian statesmen ... Dover saw them all, coming and going, winning or losing. And between those *dramatis personae* it saw an incalculable cast of nameless men and women who, having, merely a part without words, shared Milton's steadfast patience:

They also serve who only stand and wait.

Bearing west through a wide arc, I admired the prettiness of a county which Caesar called *Cantium*, from a Celtic word, *cant*, meaning either 'border' or 'coastal region'. By mutual consent the natives long ago bisected themselves into Kentish Men (who live west of the River Medway) and Men of Kent (who live east of it). Long ago, too, the county was baptised 'The Garden of England'. Celia Fiennes certainly admired the 'grass and flowers, gardens, orchards, with all sorts of herbage and tillage'. In her day the Kentish cherry orchards were a novelty, having been lately planted with Flemish saplings. In our day many of the orchards were destroyed by the cost of picking their fruit. Writing a few years after Celia Fiennes, the ubiquitous Defoe described Kent as 'the Mother of Hop-grounds in England ... where hops were planted at the beginning of the Reformation ...'. Canterbury, the capital, is Britain's senior Anglican Province or archbishopric. The city's armorial device shows a white horse above the motto *Invicta* or 'Unconquered'. That proud claim is no longer justified, because a large part of Kent has been conquered by the English themselves, as, for example, on the road from Hythe to Dungeness, which used to be a

13

country lane, but is now flanked by bungalows, caravan sites, holiday camps, and the husks of derelict houses. Dungeness was likewise littered with shacks and other of man's unsightly handiwork; but they were powerless to disturb the communion of shingle, solitude, silence, sea; all heightened by a floating bell that tolled when the waves tugged it.

Dunge Ness was the *ness* or 'headland belonging to Denge' (Old English *den-ge* or 'valley region'). This headland is the most remarkable shingle promontory in the world, formed by debris drifting from the eroded cliffs. Near to a predecessor that was built in 1904, the latest of several lighthouses contains a plaque from an earlier house, inscribed as follows: 'This lighthouse was erected by Thomas Coke Efq of Holkham Houfe in the County of Norfolk instead of the old lighthouse which originally ftood 540 yards to the northward and which by means of the land increafing from the Violence of the Sea became ufelefs to Navigation A.D. 1792. Diftant from the Sea 100 yds at low water.' At some places the beach is so steep that the five fathom and ten fathom lines almost touch each other. In the days of sail a daring captain would stand close enough for parcels to be thrown from ship to shore. Dungeness, in fact, is no place for bathers. Botanists, however, will enjoy a field day, tracing plants from bare shingle to lichened pebbles, then to a belt of scabious and cinquefoil, then of cranesbill and wood sage, then of bramble and blackthorn. It is hard going, over those pebbles. During winter the wind bites. But a salty solitude rewards the seeker.

North of Dungeness lies Romney Marsh, the only corner of Kent that remains relatively remote. The name 'Marsh' seems misleading because much of the region is rich grassland, a harvest of geological upheaval and subsidence whereby many of the Cinque Ports were left high and dry while the River Rother changed its course, and the land drove back the sea, and the Marshfolk turned their anchors into ploughshares. William Cobbett praised the Romney crops: 'I had, for the great part of the way, cornfields on one side of me and grass-land on the other . . . I never saw corn like this before'. Forty years ago, when I was a farm pupil, the Romney Marsh sheep were almost entirely free from fluke and other infectious diseases. Shepherds used to say that the sheep kept themselves immune because, instead of grazing together, they fed singly.

The Romney coast still preserves relics of the barbed wire and concrete which defied Hitler, and of the dykes and Martello towers which defied Bonaparte. For two thousand years these shores have .borne the brunt of enemy action. The Romans landed there, and after them the Jutes, Angles, Vikings, Saxons, Normans. Spain, France, and Germany aspired to land there. In World War I the Kaiser's guns shelled Kent. In World War II Hitler's guns shelled it, his aircraft bombed it, his ships waited to invade it. Time has justified Wordsworth's salutation:

Vanguard of Liberty, ye men of Kent,
Ye children of a soil that doth advance
Her haughty brow against the coast of France . . .

Whenever our young contemptibles boast that they will not defend England, they exercise a liberty which was ensured to them by the Old Contemptibles who did defend England.

But war and the rumours thereof seemed unreal while I wandered through Romney Marsh, with the sea sometimes astern, sometimes to starboard, sometimes to port; and green pastures grazed by plump sheep; and overhead the blue-and-white canopy of spring. This was a land where smugglers once carried brandy, tobacco, spices, tea, silks. But they, too, seemed as distant as Hitler and Bonaparte and the latest self-promoted Field Marshal. Presently I lay down in the sun, hearing only the larks, the sheep, and a breeze that bent the grass-blades with invisible fingers. Green, white, blue . . . they seemed to be the only colours; acres of the one, oceans of the others.

If you love quietude and the companionship of countryfolk, the Marsh is a difficult place to leave. In springtime it becomes a magnet, so that only by an effort can you detach yourself from the spaciousness, the stillness, and the sea's pervasive presence from afar. With some reluctance, therefore, I steered north via Bonnington and Woodchurch, two handsome villages; the latter possessing a hollow oak, under whose branches the medieval court leet was held.

Approaching Tenterden, I felt saddened, though not surprised, to see a ring of new houses around High Halden,

15

where I used to stay during the 1940s. The village green is still there; so also are the venerable homes and a church with a shingle broach spire; but cars encompass them, and repose has fled. I consoled myself by reflecting that few people would enjoy the life of the first occupants of those cottages, for in Merrie England a man was rated old—and lucky, too—if he lived to be sixty. When Shakespeare likened himself to autumn—'the sere and yellow'—he was about twenty-nine years old. Two centuries later, a mother felt thankful if seven of her ten children survived infancy. To weigh the past against the present is always difficult and often fruitless. Things which our grandfathers accepted as an inevitable annoyance, to us seem an avoidable ordeal. Just so, posterity may marvel that we ourselves could not eradicate the common cold; that we poisoned the air and the soil and the sea; that each year we either killed or wounded hundreds of thousands of Britons in road 'accidents'; and that while our enemies grew stronger, we chose to grow weaker, squandering borrowed money on alcohol, narcotics, and gambling.

Meanwhile, it was good to find that Tenterden had preserved much of the intimacy of a small country town. During the Middle Ages it was a Cinque Port, for the Rother could then be navigated as far inland as Bodiam, and the town's shipping lay nearby, at Smallhythe. In 1461 the Bishop of Rochester owned a quay there. Was that one of the reasons why he ordered Tenterden's thirteenth-century parish church to be topped by a tower, three hundred-and-fifty feet above the sea, which in clear weather serves as a landmark, visible from the French coast? Several local residents assured me that Tenterden was the birthplace of the father of English printing; *The Cambridge History of English Literature*, however, reserved judgement, saying only that 'William Caxton, our first printer, was born in the weald of Kent between the years 1421 and 1428, probably nearer the earlier date'. In 1455, at all events, a Thomas Caxton served as Tenterden's town clerk. It is therefore reasonable to suppose that here, or somewhere not far off, was born the boy who in 1438 became apprenticed to a London cloth merchant, whence he migrated to the Low Countries, spending some years in the service of the Duchess of Burgundy. At Cologne, for the first time in his life, he saw a printing press. Soon afterwards he acquired one, and eventually published from Bruges the first book in the English language, his own translation of *Recuvell of the Histories of Troy*. Returning to England in 1476, he set up his press at a house within the precincts of Westminster Abbey. Nineteen years later he died, having printed and, in some instances, translated several classics, including St Jerome's *Lives of the Fathers*, Malory's *Morte d'Arthur*, and Gower's *Confessio Amantis* (which contained an early example of a printer's error, dating itself 1493 instead of 1483). Thomas Caxton's influence on literature was not confined to the printing press. By translating books into English, he furthered the example of Langland and Chaucer, who chose to write in the vernacular rather than in Latin or French.

'The pen,' boasted Lord Lytton, 'is mightier than the sword.' But he omitted to say which pen and whose sword. Despite much meandering, my journey led toward a man whose fame was written with ink *and* with blood. In order to reach that fame, I followed a lane which confirmed that Kent is still a garden of fruit and flowers. Through hopfields I went, those birthplaces of beer, staked and criss-crossed like a mammoth crop of sweet peas. Beside the lane stood farmsteads where that beer was once brewed in an oasthouse (Old English *ast*, meaning 'to burn'). Many of the farmsteads had ceased to farm; many of the oasthouses were incorporated as part of the main building, or enlarged and modernised as weekend cottages; yet how warmly they glowed in the evening sun; their lawns like a billiard table; the windows picked-out in white; the tiled roof of each oasthouse tilting rakishly like a gnome's cap.

Approaching the Sussex border, I confronted a fact that was to follow me throughout my journey, the variety of the English landscape, which differs not only from county to county but also within each county, so that South Devon is seen to differ from North Devon, even as industrial Lancashire differs from Lakeland Lancashire. Many of those differences are vivid and therefore immediately perceptible; others are subtle and, to a stranger, indiscernible. How, for example, does .one define the nuances which distinguish West Kent from East Sussex? Both regions contain hopfields, oasthouses, weatherboarding, hills, woods, pastures. Insofar as they retain it, both speak a dialect.

And neither has escaped the tentacles of London. Yet the differences between them exist and must be analysed. Myself, I never become aware of the differences simply by crossing from Kent to Sussex. I must travel at least half-dozen miles in order to detect a feature that says 'Sussex'. Sure enough, I found one, at a point where the lane reached a crossroads with a signpost to Battle; and there, on the horizon, lay the remnant of a weald or forest, stretching from east to west, far as the eye could see. A forest, of course, is not necessarily a wood. It may be any large tract of wild country. But the Sussex Weald really was a wood, until commerce felled it.

Sussex, the land of the South Saxons, is divided into three regions: Weald, Downs, coast. At Whatlington, a mile or two beyond the crossroads, I was in the Weald, or what remained of it. In 1586 William Camden's *Britannia* mentioned 'an opinion that some men maintain concerning this Weald, which is, that it was a great while altogether in a manner nothing else than a desert and waste wilderness, not planted with towns or peopled with men, as the outsides of the shire were, but stored and stuffed with herds of deer and droves of hogs only'. Toward the end of the Middle Ages the Wealden huntsmen and swineherds gave way to hamlets that were enlarged by the Flemish weavers whom Edward III imported, and after them by the native woodsmen and ironsmelters. The Romans had made crude attempts at smelting, but the English became so skilful that their furnaces ultimately devoured most of the trees. By the middle of the sixteenth century, Queen Elizabeth was forced to restrict felling lest the Navy found itself without timber for ships. Seven years after the Queen's death, Sussex still contained 140 forges, burning 1,790 trees every week throughout the year. In 1651 the forges began to use coke, but by that time a vast area of woodland had been destroyed. When the last Sussex furnace closed down—at Ashburnham in 1828—most of the Weald had become farmland.

One of the memorials to the old forest lay in the parish of Burwash, only a few miles from where I stood. It was a large house, named Bateman's, built by a retired ironmaster in 1634. Three centuries later, Rudyard Kipling bought it, enlarged and improved the grounds, and found there his heart's desire:

Each to his choice, and I rejoice
The lot has fallen to me . . .
Yea, Sussex by the sea!

Kipling lived at Bateman's for nearly thirty-five years, and his widow gave the estate to the National Trust.

Meanwhile, I was still at Whatlington, a one-shop hamlet astride the Hastings road, several miles short of the aforementioned man of blood-and-ink. Yet I lingered, partly to admire a wooded landscape climbing skyhigh above Mountfield, and partly to quiz a Wesleyan chapel carrying not only a spire (a vanity seldom indulged by dissenters) but also a sign, *Antiques*. Venturing inside, I found oak coffers, Chippendale chairs, Persian rugs, and clocks hallmarked by history. Yet in that same building, though never amid such beauty, had worshipped those sons and daughters of the soil for whom the chapel was a stairway to salvation and a snub to the Establishment.

Refreshed by the brief sojourn among English craftsmanship, I continued along a winding lane, flanked by several dignified houses. After about two miles I reached at last the site of the most famous battle in English history, commonly called the Battle of Hastings despite the fact that it was fought seven miles inland, at a place which the victors re-named *La Bataille* or 'Battle'. Battle is a small country town with many ancient buildings, notably a medieval house on the Whatlington lane, crazily unsymmetrical. As at Tenterden, most of the residents are either retired or engaged in urban affairs. Seldom do you meet gaitered farmers speaking a local dialect. Nevertheless, Battle is a rural place—bustling but not deafening—and from the heights above it you can box a compass of wooded hills. Cobbett spoke wisely when he said that his choice of an ideal home 'has always been very much between the woods of Sussex and the downs of Wiltshire'.

Here, then, occurred the event which Professor Freeman called The Battle of Senlac, a word that survives as a local placename (Old English *sand-lacu* or 'sandy brook'). Not many Englishmen understand the significance of that battle, nor the adventures of the man who lost it, Harold, son of the rebellious Earl of Wessex, a claimant to the English throne. Having

19

inherited the earldom, Harold was shipwrecked off the French coast, and became a prisoner of the Duke of Normandy, who likewise coveted the English throne. There is a tradition that—in order to regain his freedom—Harold vowed to relinquish his own claim; but we know very little about the alleged incident, because none of the contemporary English chroniclers mentioned it. Our only sources are some remarks by Norman scribes, and a detail from the Bayeux Tapestry, showing Harold between two altars, on each of which stands a reliquary. After his release, Harold did seize the English throne. Several years later, during the autumn of 1066, Duke William of Normandy landed with an army at Pevensey. Three weeks previously, unknown to the Duke, King Harold had defeated a body of Norwegian invaders at Stamford Bridge in Yorkshire. Within less than a fortnight, however, he marched two hundred miles to London; spent six days settling affairs of State; and then marched sixty miles into Sussex, where the Normans were encamped.

At dawn on Saturday, 14 October 1066, Harold deployed his men on the height called Senlac. The English in those years possessed no standing army. Their force consisted of seven thousand conscripts or feudal levies, stiffened by the King's bodyguard of House-Carles. The Normans numbered about the same, but were superior in armoured cavalry. William, who had either to advance on London or to retreat into the Channel, moved inland from Hastings. When he sighted the English he vowed that, if he defeated them, he would build an abbey on the battlefield. At about nine o'clock in the morning, to the sound of trumpets and war-cries, the invaders charged uphill. All day their cavalry rode in vain against the English infantry. The Duke had three horses killed under him. The King, wielding a doublehanded sword, was covered with wounds. Then, as the sun began to set, William saw that Time had turned against him. A retreat would become a disaster. He therefore told his archers to aim in the air, hoping that their volleys would fall on the heads of the English. The stratagem succeeded. Harold, in fact, was blinded by an arrow. Despite his agony, he continued to fight until he was surrounded and hacked to pieces. Demoralised, the English conscripts fled, but the King's bodyguard fought on until not one of them remained alive.

Two months later, on Christmas Day 1066, in Westminster Abbey, the Duke of Normandy was crowned King of England; and for more than a century thereafter the Normans dominated the land. Some of their architecture has survived, and with it some relics of a feudal system that was already in existence when they landed. But of their language our own bears little trace. William Langland wrote *Piers the Plowman* in the vernacular. Chaucer, too, wrote in his native tongue, and never more concisely than when he described a poet's lifelong apprenticeship:

> The lyf so short, the craft so long to learne,
> Th'assay so hard, so sharp the conquering . . .

Greatly outnumbered by their subject people, the Normans never eradicated Englishry, though Englishry itself became a badge of servitude, for the conquerors exacted from Englishmen a corporate fine whenever any one was murdered in their village or hundred. If, however, the villagers could prove that the dead man was English, then, by invoking the Presentment of Englishry, they were exempt from the fine; so lightly did the conquerors value the lives of the conquered.

Meanwhile, after his victory, William fulfilled the vow he had made before the battle. A great abbey began to arise on the site, and was blessed by the Bishop of Chichester in 1076. Eighteen years later it was consecrated in the presence of the Conqueror's son, William II. When the monasteries were dissolved, Henry VIII gave Battle Abbey to his Master of Horse, Sir Anthony Browne, who acquired another Sussex seat, Cowdray Park near Midhurst. The abbey church at Battle has almost entirely disappeared, but some of the monastic buildings survive and are part of a girls' school. In 1976 the abbey and the battlefield were offered for sale at a price not far short of a million pounds sterling. Since no private buyer was likely to afford such a sum, local residents appealed for funds to rescue the national heritage from commercial 'development'. In the end, the land was acquired largely by the generosity of anonymous Americans who presented it to the nation that scarcely deserved it.

Battle during the eighteenth century gave substance to its

martial name. 'Battle,' said Defoe, 'is remarkable . . . for making the finest gun-powder, and the best perhaps in Europe . . .'. Even today the parish bears several symbolic scars. South-east of the abbey, for example, a field is called Mal Fosse or 'Evil Ditch' because many Normans were buried there after the fight. Beyond Mal Fosse, near Telham Hill, an ancient yew tree is said to mark the place where Duke William deployed his army.

The road from Battle to Heathfield crosses a beautiful countryside. The hills are tall enough to seem high; the valleys yield much wheat, meat, fleece, fruit. The old houses are less heavily timbered than those in Kent, but not less handsome. Yet one is all the while conscious of too many people, too many bungalows, too many cars. Is this the land which a twentieth-century essayist, E. V. Lucas, described as 'that inaccessible and alluring country'? Alluring it remains, among the less populous parts, but no longer inaccessible, for cars have completed a conquest which railways began: London to Brighton in 1841, London to Worthing in 1845, London to St Leonards in 1848, London to Hastings in 1850. Professor J. A. Williams set the south-eastern scene when he said that a large part of it had been conquered 'by the swelling flood of detribalised people from no particular region, the hotel-keepers, *rentiers*, holiday-makers, who constitute the amorphous society of modern England . . .'.

Near a place called Woods Corner I ventured along a favourite bylane, away from the traffic. The sky was as blue as May could paint, and on it sailed six white clouds. Northward I saw a rampart of hills, and a glint of water, and several redbrick farms, and one church tower rising like a grey and leafless tree, and smoke-wisps from bonfires, and dollops of creamy sheep, and cattle like polished boots; all creating a landscape praised by a Sussex squire and poet, William Scawen Blunt:

> Dear checker woods, the Sussex Weald!
> If a name thrills me yet of things of earth,
> That name is thine . . .

From Heathfield my route led north-west into Uckfield (an ugly, overgrown town) and thence through Haywards Heath (an overgrown, ugly town) into Cuckfield, whose name may mean a field either of couch-grass (Old English *cwice*) or of cuckoos

(Latin *cuculus*). I preferred the latter name because it was at cuckoo-time that I first saw Cuckfield, in years when cars were few and courteous. Up and down the steep street I strolled, observing that each house, instead of being a copy of its neighbour, reflected the identities of the men who built it and of the families who occupied it. So, once again, I was in Cuckfield at cuckoo-time, though the bird itself went unheard above the traffic. At a first glance the village seemed scarcely to have changed in forty years. The few perceptible additions were for the better, and could be seen in the well nourished residents, the hygienic shops, the modern sanitation. But, of course, Cuckfield had changed so drastically that I doubted whether it now contained a dozen people who worked on the land, or as wheelwrights, masons, farriers, carpenters, seedsmen, gamekeepers. Cuckfield had become a haven for pensioners and commuters. In it, therefore, I faced a sign of the times, and decided to state it frankly, if only in order to avoid tedious repetitions.

Thus, until the beginning of the twentieth century an average English village was founded on four facts: first, the majority of villagers worked either on the land or as ancillaries to those who did so work; second, the villagers were numbered rather in hundreds than in thousands, and never at all in several thousands; third, the villagers travelled either on foot or in a horse-drawn vehicle; fourth, the villagers seldom travelled far or frequently, being by nature and occupation what Gilbert White described as 'stationary men'. Whether such people were happier than modern villagers is debatable and for the moment irrelevant. It will do to state those four facts and then to emphasise the extent to which they have been outdated: first, in many villages the majority of people no longer work on the land; second, in many villages the people *are* numbered in several thousands; third, the majority of villagers do *not* travel either on foot or in a horse-drawn vehicle; fourth, the majority of villagers *do* travel far and frequently. To ignore them those changes, or to assume that they occurred long ago, is to overlook the upheavals which transformed the rhythm and pattern of English country life during the second half of the twentieth century.

En route for Horsham and the Surrey border, I made a detour

into Shipley, the home of Hilaire Belloc, who, with Kipling and Blunt, formed the *tres magi* of twentieth-century Sussex. Born in France, of a French father and of an English mother, Joseph Peter René Hilaire Belloc was a notable example of *de facto* Englishry. When Madame Belloc's husband died prematurely, she moved with her son to Sussex. Years later, while serving as a conscript with the French artillery, Hilaire Belloc dreamed of his English childhood: 'I remembered Sussex,' he wrote, 'and the woods above Arun, and I felt myself to be in exile'. Ultimately he became a naturalised British subject. As a scholar of Balliol, he hoped to win the Fellowship which would enable him to follow his true vocation as historian, essayist, and poet. That hope was not fulfilled; so—in order to support his wife and children—he turned to politics and journalism. Between 1903 and 1906 he published eleven books and pamphlets, as well as reams of newspaper articles. In 1906 his wife told a friend: 'We have bought a place of our own in Sussex. A lovely old long brick house'. This house—at one time a village shop—was called King's Land, and with it went five acres and a windmill. The oldest parts were built six centuries ago; the newest, in 1890. The Bellocs dined in a stone-flagged room, warmed by logs on an open hearth. Their oak refectory table, once the property of St John's College, Oxford, was bought for £10. As at Bateman's, so at King's Land; a poet lived there until his death many years later, and in it sang the praises of Sussex. Despite his labours, Belloc never grew rich. In 1938, when he was nearly eighty years old, he published either a book or a pamphlet every two months. Yet amid the journeywork shine some of the finest prose and most beautiful lyrics in modern English literature. In *Four Just Men* he became a guide to Sussex as it was before cars conquered it. In *The Path to Rome* he became a pilgrim. In *The Voyage of the Nona* he became a Channel pilot, disillusioned by this world, yet, as a Roman Catholic, trusting in another: 'of all creatures that move and breathe upon the earth we of mankind are the fullest of sorrows. But the sea shall comfort us, and perpetually show us new things and assure us. It is the sacrament of the world. May it be to others what it has been to me'.

From Sussex, the land of the *Suth Seaxe*, I reached Surrey, the land of the *Suthrigs*. Those parts of the county which lie furthest from London are worth visiting; notably Frensham (near the Hampshire border) and Lingfield (near the Sussex border). Elsewhere the traveller is conscious of entering a rustic suburb, for Surrey was the first victim of London's transport. My own route was condemned to follow parts of a race track whereon the going became so gruesome that, in order to survive, I looked neither to the right nor to the left, but stared unblinking at the vehicle ahead, and sometimes via a mirror at the maniac astern. In Shalford (the Norman *Scaldeford* or 'shallow ford') I stopped to explore the village green where my sister and I once played when we were children. The green was still there, but in order to reach it I had to wait until a gap in the traffic allowed me to cross the road. The old watermill, they told me, had been restored and given to the National Trust by a group of anonymous benefactors. It is an eighteenth-century three-pair mill overlooking the River Tillingbourne. The lower parts are of brick; the two upper storeys, hung with red tiles, are framed in chestnut and oak, filled with brick nogging. Despite the traffic, Shalford watermill reminded me of Flatford Mill in Suffolk. If you have seen such a place, you will understand why Constable felt happy whenever, as he said, he found himself 'surrounded by weirs, backwaters, nets and willows, with the smell of weeds, flowing water and flour . . .'.

Watermills are an ancient feature of the English scene. Thirty-five years before the Romans first invaded Britain, a Latin writer, Vitruvius, described what he called his 'new invention' or watermill. Domesday Book mentions 5,624 such mills. During the Middle Ages they were controlled by the Admiralty officials who might demolish any mill that impeded navigation. In 1442 the control passed to a Commissioner of Sewers, but no one was ever able to eradicate the disputes. In 1816 a civil engineer, John Sutcliffe, wrote: 'In consequence of so many water-mills, the country is never free from litigation and vexations, lawsuits respecting erecting, repairing, or raising weirs, by which the peace and harmony of neighbours and friends are often destroyed'. Despite much bickering, the watermills prospered because they were needed. In 1936 a rural survey remarked: 'Up to 50 years ago it was customary for villages in parts of Bedfordshire to sow part of their gardens with corn which the

25

miller ground for them, keeping the bran and returning the flour'. In 1948 the watermill at Ashrigg in Yorkshire was generating electricity for a large area of Swaledale. In 1977 a watermill was generating electricity for a cottage near Brayford in Devon.

From Shalford Mill I made toward Bagshot Heath, which used to lie within Windsor Great Park, and was frequented by highwaymen. Celia Fiennes complained that the road across the Heath was 'a heavy sandy way'. Modern geologists would point to the gravel or Bagshot Beds which give the district an outcrop of scrubland. Cobbett cited an area not far from Guildford 'where the gravel is so near the top as not to suffer even the heath to grow'. He allowed, however, that Surrey was not everywhere barren: 'It has some of the very best and some of the very worst land, not only in England but in the world'.

In 1912 a Surrey wheelwright, George Bourne, published *Change in the Village*, which told how Surrey became a London suburb: 'during the last ten years,' Bourne stated, 'the valley has been "discovered" as a "residential centre". A water-company gave the signal for development. No sooner was a good water-supply available than speculating architects and builders began to buy up vacant plots of land, or even cottages ... the final shabby patches of heath are disappearing; on all hands glimpses of new buildings and raw new roads defy you to persuade yourself that you are in a country place. In fact, the place is a suburb ... and the once-quiet highway is noisy with the motor-cars of the richer residents and all the town traffic ...'. Only among the very old people will you hear what George Bourne heard: 'a man rolling out his *Nice mornin'* with the fat Surrey "R".'

It was during a traffic-jam that I suddenly remembered William the Conqueror and the Domesday Book wherewith the pen proved itself mightier—or at any rate less rusty—than the sword. In 1086, twenty years after his victory at *La Bataille*, William commissioned a 'Description of All England' that would provide an accurate and comprehensive estimate of the political and economic state of his new kingdom. Despite its title, Domesday Book did not cover 'All England'. The far north, for instance, had defied the Normans, and was so devastated by

26

them as to seem not worth surveying. The south-west of England was covered by an Exon Domesday, for which the returns were made by a dozen jurors from each hundred of Dorset, Wiltshire, Somerset, Devonshire, Cornwall. Nevertheless, the greater part of England was visited by four commissioners with power to summon sheriffs, barons, priests, reeves, and indeed any man who could state on oath and from his own knowledge how the land had been held during the reign of Edward the Confessor, and how it was held in 1086. The commissioners recorded the names of the principal landowners together with the number of their plough-teams, cattle, horses, sheep, pigs, mills, pastures, woodlands, fish-ponds, and other relevant details. They recorded also the value of each manor in 1066 and in 1086. According to the Bishop of Hereford, the returns were checked by a second body of commissioners. The natives themselves resented such intrusion. Some of them resisted it, and were killed during disputes. All likened it to the Last Judgement or Day of Doom. In 1179 the Treasurer of England wrote: 'This book is called by the natives Domesday—that is, metaphorically speaking, the day of judgement'. The Treasurer was referring to the Book of Revelation: 'And I saw the dead, small and great, stand before God; and the books were opened; and another book was opened, which is the book of life: and the dead were judged out of those things which were written in the books, according to their works'.

This remarkable census was compiled within less than one year. The rolls of parchment, on which it was written in Latin by royal clerks, formed two volumes; one covering the southern and midland shires, the other covering Essex, Norfolk, and Suffolk. The entire record was then preserved in the Royal Treasury at Winchester. Like the Paston Letters, though on a wider and deeper scale, Domesday Book is invaluable to historians. No other nation possesses anything comparable. In that sense, therefore, William's achievement with the pen was indeed more lasting than his prowess with a sword.

Eventually the traffic dwindled, and the houses receded. White gates appeared, leading to gravel drives flanked by rhododendrons. Victorian Gothick loomed above high walls while Edwardian Tudor held a not-too-neighbourly *tête-à-tête*

27

with Atomic Cubism. 'This,' I decided, 'must be Ascot.' It was. And after it, came fields and trees and deer. In short, I had reached Windsor Great Park where, by gracious permission of Her Majesty the Queen, I was at liberty to wander among five thousand acres.

Windsor Great Park is largely a creation of the Duke of Cumberland, who, having commanded an army in the Low Countries in 1747, resolved on his return to find employment for the demobilised soldiers. At his own cost he made extensive alterations to the Park, in which he was assisted by the deputy ranger, Thomas Sandby, and his brother Paul, each of whom became a founder member of the Royal Academy. Their only failure was zoological rather than horticultural, for they introduced several lions and tigers to the Park, one of which killed an eight-year-old child; whereafter the beasts were banished to the Tower of London. Unfortunately, the traffic on the roads through the Park has destroyed the repose which Pastor Moritz found in 1782: 'I went,' he wrote, 'down a gentle slope to Windsor Park, wherein the dim light surrounds you like the atmosphere of a temple. This forest surpasses anything you can imagine of this sort, for to its natural charms were added the peace of solitude, the cool evening air and soft music coming from the distant castle'.

Defoe, you remember, warned the readers of his travelogue that 'antiquity is not my search in this work . . .'. But at Windsor Castle he changed his tune: 'And now I am, by just degrees, come to Windsor where I must leave talking of trade, river, navigation, meal and malt, and describe the most beautiful, the most pleasantly situated castle and royal palace, in the whole of Britain'. If you reach Windsor at noon on a sunny day you will find crowds, cars, cacophony, and not much else. If you reach Windsor early on a weekday you will find a steep little town overlooking Britain's premier river and premier school.

Windsor—a *windlesora* or 'landing place'—achieved importance when William the Conqueror built a castle there, which Henry I converted into a palace. Nothing of those buildings has survived. The present castle is an amalgam of styles from the fourteenth to the nineteenth century. Thus, the Round Tower was built by Henry II, and the castle walls were enlarged by Edward III, who added three towers. St George's Chapel was the work of Edward IV, Henry VII, Henry VIII. Queen Elizabeth I built the North Terrace and above it a gallery. Charles II renovated the State Apartments. George IV commissioned Wyatt to build new features and to modify some of the old. William IV removed a potentially dangerous gas installation; replaced the German band with an ensemble of English players; presented an assortment of animals to the new London Zoo; built cottages for estate workers; and admitted the public onto the castle terrace. Prince Albert not only designed a model farm and dairy but also improved the security precautions after an intruder had stolen and published Queen Victoria's sketch-book ... an incident castigated by *The Times*: 'Let the QUEEN of Great Britain be able to sit down to her piano or sketch-book with the same security against intrusion as any other lady in the land'.

Were I asked to name one feature of the castle that most deeply stirs the imagination, I would choose St George's Chapel, the shrine of the Most Noble Order of the Garter, a chivalrous brotherhood founded by King Edward I to celebrate his victory at Crécy, where an English army of 13,000 defeated 40,000 men led by the Kings of France, of Bohemia, of Moravia, and of the Romans. During the battle the young Prince of Wales and a number of knights were surrounded and in great peril. A messenger was sent, begging for reinforcements; but the King refused to throw in his last reserves: 'Let the boy win his spurs'. On returning home, the King commemorated his triumph by founding the Most Noble Order of the Garter for the Sovereign and twenty-six knights, 'the valyantest men of the realm', each being linked to the rest by vows for the advancement of piety, nobility, and chivalry: 'Tie about thy leg for thy renown this Noble Garter; wear it as a symbol of the most illustrious Order, never to be forgotten or laid aside, that thereby thou mayest be admonished to be courageous, and, having undertaken a just war ... that thou mayest stand firm, and valiantly and successfully conquer'. The Order's badge was a replica of a garter which the Countess of Salisbury accidentally dropped during a ball at Calais. Historians have confirmed the truth of a tradition that the King retrieved the fallen garter and then tied it round his own knee, exclaiming: '*Honi soit qui mal y pense*'.

Like the Order of Merit and the Royal Victorian Order, the Garter is bestowed solely at the Sovereign's behest. It remains Britain's greatest official distinction of a kind altogether different from the 'Honours' that are nowadays scattered like confetti. Samuel Pepys was deeply moved when he and his wife were conducted over the Knights' Chapel by the organist: 'So took coach to Windsor . . . and thither sent for Dr. Childe, who come to us and carried us to St. George's Chapel and there placed us among the Knights' stalls . . . and hither come cushions to us, and a young singing-boy to bring us a copy of the anthem to be sung. And here, for our sakes, had this anthem and the great service sung, extraordinarily, only to entertain us. It is a noble place indeed, and a Quire of good voice . . . After prayers, we to see the plate of the chapel, and the robes of the Knights, and a man to show us the banners of the several Knights in being, which hang above the stalls'.

Windsor's domestic architecture is chiefly Victorian, Edwardian and Welfare. The town hall, however, was completed by Sir Christopher Wren, from the design of an architect who died in harness. Wren's father had been Dean of Windsor, and the son became one of the town's two members of parliament (the pair being halved in 1867). An hotel near the bridge carries a plaque: 'This house was built and occupied by Sir Christopher Wren 1676'. Despite diligent search, I have failed to verify that claim.

Windsor lies in Berkshire, a Royal County on the south bank of the Thames. Facing it, on the northern bank, lies Buckinghamshire, and in it Eton College, founded by King Henry VI, whose charter decreed that the College should consist of a Provost, ten Fellows, four clerks, six choristers, a schoolmaster, twenty-five poor scholars, and twenty-five infirm old men. Free instruction in grammar was given to an indefinite number of poor boys from any part of the world. As all the world now knows, the College prospered and grew large, though never to the exclusion of its poor scholars. For more than five hundred years King Henry's College at Eton has played a pre-eminent role in English history and therefore in world history. No other school can claim such a roll-call of premiers, lords-chancellors, foreign secretaries, archbishops, bishops, poets, judges, and leaders of the armed forces. The Etonian top hats and tailcoats add two-old-penceworth of colour to the plainness of a one-new-penny world. Recalling its impact on his own childhood, Robert Bridges evoked the venerable youthfulness of this famous school:

Here is eternal spring; for you
The very stars of heaven are new;
And agèd fame again is born
Fresh as the peeping flowers at morn.

There remains the river, Milton's 'royal-towered Thames'. How stately it flows at Windsor, carving a wide arc among meadows. Caesar called it *Tamesis*; Tacitus called it *Tamesa*; and both names come from *Tamasa* (a tributary of the Ganges), meaning 'dark river' or, more precisely, a river whose muddy soil causes the water to seem less 'light' than that of rivers with a pebbly bottom. Rising from a field near Coates in Gloucestershire, and ending as an estuary near Gravesend in Essex, the Thames has witnessed more history than have all our other rivers put together. The Tower of London, Whitehall, Hampton Court, Runnymede, Windsor Castle, Oxford (a seat of Parliament and Kings) . . . these felt the very pulse of England; and below them, in the Pool of London and the Port of London, many ships unloaded their news of the world. England is unique among large islands in possessing so many navigable rivers. Sicily has none, nor have Crete, Cyprus, Sardinia, Corsica, and Iceland.

Between its source and Teddington Lock—where the waters are non-tidal—the Thames comes under the control of the Thames Water Authority, formerly the Thames Conservancy Board. Below Teddington—where the waters are tidal and tinged with brine—the Thames comes under the control of the Port of London Authority. For centuries a commercial highway, the river above Teddington seldom carries a barge. On the lower reaches the dwindling traffic recalls Pepys's lament when plague struck the city: 'But Lord! what a sad time it is to see no boats upon the River . . .'. Swans, however, ply their lawful occasions, being royal birds and therefore subject to royal governance. During the Middle Ages no subject might lawfully keep swans on open and common water without the King's consent. The ancient office of Master of the King's Game of Swans still survives. Most of the Thames swans belong to the Crown; the rest are owned by two City companies, the Vintners and the Dyers, who acquired the right to keep swans centuries ago, probably because their offices or halls stood close to the river. Every summer the pageant of swan-upping brings colour to the scene when officials representing the Crown and the two companies row in six boats from the Pool of London to Henley-on-Thames, wearing white trousers, woollen caps, and striped jerseys. En route they count and mark the swans. Since 1910 the royal swans have been exempt from marking. All other mature swans or 'clear-bills' receive one or two nicks on their side or on their mandible, signifying that they belong to one of the two companies.

Beachy Head, Sussex
Beachy Head stands five hundred and seventy-five feet above the English Channel or Shakespeare's Moat. Three centuries ago the Marquess of Halifax warned the English that 'human rights' and 'social justice' will not long survive in a nation which refuses to defend itself. 'The first Article in an Englishman's Political Creed,' he wrote, 'must be, that he believeth in the Sea . . .'. We are an island still, and over the sea comes the bulk of our material nourishment.

Beachy Head was not named after the beach. Medieval Englishmen called it *Beau Chef* or 'Beautiful Head'. Built in 1912, the lighthouse sends a beam twenty miles seaward. The wind here is seldom still and never scentless. If it blows from the south, said Richard Jefferies, 'the waves refine it; if inland, the wheat and flowers and grass distil it'. Kipling spanned the centuries when he described this famous coastline:

Clean of officious fence or hedge,
Half-wild and wholly tame,
The wise turf cloaks the white cliff edge
As when the Romans came.

Every Englishman ought to make use of the steamers that ply between London and Oxford. Above Windsor he will find a crescendo of beauty via Cliveden Reach to Henley-on-Thames, where the Chiltern beechwoods come down to the water's edge. Above Reading he will find an adagio of quietude via Matthew Arnold's 'stripling Thames' to Lechlade in Gloucestershire. Above Lechlade a canoe may proceed for another mile or so, sharing Laurence Binyon's water music:

> And the lonely stream hiding
> Shy birds, grew more lonely,
> And with us was only
> The noise of our gliding.

For me on this journey the Thames at Windsor was a Rubicon. Having crossed it, I approached the South Midlands.

Milton Street, Sussex

Blue skies, white clouds, brown furrows, and an ebony etching of winter trees; beyond them, the Downs; and beyond the Downs, the sea. Those are some of the reasons why Hilaire Belloc declared:

> I will build a house with a deep thatch
> To shelter me from the cold,
> And there shall the Sussex songs be sung
> And the story of Sussex told.

Milton Street was the Old English *mylen-tun* or 'mill town' near a *straet* or 'Roman road'. During the 1860s a hoard of Saxon coins was found at Milton Street, not surprisingly, because Sussex was the cradle of Saxon England as well as one of the landfalls of Roman invaders.

Nearby, at Alfriston, the large church is called 'The Cathedral of the Downs'. The priest's house (*c.*1350) was the first property ever to be bought by the National Trust.

3 THE SOUTH MIDLANDS

The shire was created by the King of Wessex more than a thousand years ago. Derived from the Old English *scir* or 'administrative office', the word came to mean the region administered by that office, and more especially a group of hundreds or wapentakes ruled jointly by an earldorman and a shire reeve or sheriff. With the exceptions of Northumberland, Durham, Cumberland, Westmorland, Lancashire, and Rutland, all the English counties existed before the Norman Conquest. In 1974, however, many of the ancient boundaries were either altered or obliterated, and a large number of local councils were abolished, leaving villagers to the mercy of strangers in a distant town. This was done in the name of 'efficiency'.

A different type of 'efficiency' confronted me at Slough, the Saxon *sloh*, 'a quagmire' or place to be avoided. Alas, Slough cannot be avoided by anyone wishing to pass from Windsor to the Chiltern Hills, unless, like Chesterton, he chooses to go by way of Beachy Head. Slough consists of cars, lorries, carriageways ... factories, pylons, power houses ... noise, speed, money. Fortunately, the Babel possesses one great merit; you can escape from it quickly. Within a matter of minutes, therefore, I reached Stoke Poges and the most famous country churchyard in Britain:

> The curfew tolls the knell of parting day,
> The lowing herd wind slowly o'er the lea,
> The plowman homeward plods his weary way,
> And leaves the world to darkness and to me.

It was on 12 June 1750 that Thomas Gray completed the poem which he had conceived and partly composed seven years earlier, *Elegy Written in a Country Churchyard*, the greatest of its kind in English literature. Gray sent the manuscript to his friend, Horace Walpole, who showed it to the editor of the *Magazine of Magazines*, who informed Gray that he proposed to print it. Gray himself—an academic recluse—disliked piracy even more than he shunned publicity. He therefore presented the copyright gratis to Dodsley, a publisher, declaring that no gentleman could write for money; an opinion which Dodsley hastened to approve. Gray stipulated, however, that his poem be published anonymously. Fifteen editions appeared within eleven years, from which the publisher made much money, and the poet none at all. But, as Joseph Conrad observed, 'an artist's richest treasure lies in the hearts of men and women'. Gray's authorship soon became known, and his genius has ever after been acknowledged. 'As an elegiac poet,' declared Swinburne, 'Gray holds for all ages to come, his unassailable sovereign situation.' Nor was that opinion shared only by literary men. A few hours before General Wolfe scaled the Heights of Abraham, he recited aloud a large part of the *Elegy*, including its tribute to Hodge, the collective name for English hinds or farmhands:

Far from the madding crowd's ignoble strife
Their sober wishes never learn'd to stray;
Along the cool sequester'd vale of life
They kept the noiseless tenor of their way.

Having recited, Wolfe made a remark to one of his officers, which was overheard and copied down by Professor Robinson, who at that time served as a recruit: 'I would,' said Wolfe, 'prefer being the author of that Poem to the glory of beating the French tomorrow'.

Stoke Poges is the *stoc* or 'place' whose lord in 1255 was Hubert le Pugeis. When Gray lived there with his mother, he called the place 'a hamlet'. Today it is a suburb of London and Slough. The famous churchyard stands close to a manor house that was built for the Earl of Huntingdon, Master of the Horse to Mary Tudor. Charles I was imprisoned there by the rebels. The house ultimately passed to the Penn family, one of whom erected a monument to Gray, not far from his tomb.

After Stoke Poges I soon sighted the Chilterns, a range of chalk hills stretching southward from Hertfordshire to the

Thames at Hambleden in Buckinghamshire, and westward from Dunstable in Bedfordshire to Ewelme in Oxfordshire. At their highest point the Chilterns stand nearly a thousand feet above the sea. From time immemorial their beechwoods and combes or 'bottoms' were a haunt of criminals. During the Middle Ages a stewardship of the Chiltern Hundreds was established to suppress the outlaws, many of whom were publicly hanged (witness Hangings Lane in Prestwood and Gallows Hill near Ellesborough). Today the stewardship enjoys a political fame whose origins can be traced to the year 1623, when Parliament more or less forbade any member of the Commons to resign his seat. This was done because members were apt to resign when their duty as politicians clashed with their responsibility as landowners. In 1707 Parliament countered royal patronage (a polite name for bribery) by requiring a member of the Commons to resign his seat if he accepted 'an office of profit under the Crown'. In 1750 it so happened that the member for Wareham wished to stand for a neighbouring constituency. Bearing in mind the Acts of 1623 and 1707, he decided that the stewardship of the Chiltern Hundreds, which had long since become a sinecure, would disbar him from sitting in the Commons, but without imposing new duties; so, having accepted the stewardship, he resigned his seat, then resigned the stewardship, and finally stood as candidate for Dorchester.

Despite prolonged felling and widespread 'development' the Chiltern beechwoods are still famous. 'Here,' wrote Defoe, 'is also brought down a vast quantity of beech wood, which grows in Buckinghamshire more plentifully than in any other part of England . . . without which, the City of London would be put to more difficulty, than for any other thing of its kind in the nation.' Chiltern furniture was made by bodgers or cottage craftsmen, several of whom worked in a tent among the woods, turning chair legs on a pole-lathe. Bodgers did not become extinct until the mid-twentieth century. I last met one in 1943, while walking home at night through Coppice Wood near Great Hampden. I can remember my astonishment at seeing a ghostly light shining behind a canopy of white sheets. Inside, a bodger was at work. I still have the notes I made while sitting in his tent: 'He turns chair legs on a primitive pole lathe for Wycombe factory. Also makes furniture for people who pay a little extra in return for objects that look a lot better than mass-productions. Farmers employ him to mend gates, barn doors, chick-sheds etc. Also works with Hampden blacksmith mending wagons, wheels etc. Pays the Earl's agent a few shillings a year for right to fell quota of beech. We drank cocoa heated over a fire of wood chips. Got home 10 pm'.

I used to live among the Chilterns, in a hilltop house beside a cart-track ending at a wood. The old farmhand who milked cows in the meadow spoke a vernacular that was partly unintelligible to other counties. This multiplicity of regional accents and regional words is unique. No other nation possesses such a wide variety within so small a compass. Despite radio and television, almost every English county preserves traces of a local intonation. In the more secluded parts of the Chilterns you may still hear a few local words, such as *pimmocky* or 'fastidious', *kurlick* or 'charlock', *slommakin* or 'slovenly'. A wise man loves the language of his youth, and in it hears the voice of variety adding spice to life: 'Bert's a-drove thart there 'ole steam-roller. Roight up th'oigh street 'ee went. Fair pissing along, as you moight say. So oi said to 'im arterwards, "Bert, boy," oi said, "oi never thought as oi'd live to see a trarkshun injin puffing through the middle o' Missenden again. Oi thought them things was where oi'm bound for . . . the scrap 'eap." But Bert wouldn't 'ave none o' thart. "Not on your life," says 'ee, "These 'ere trarkshuns is all the rage nowadays. Any silly bastard as can spend fifty quid on a ton o' coal takes 'isself for a roide at Gawd-knows-ow-much-a-moile. Heighteen noinety-four this 'ere were built, and oi'm telling you, boy, she shot up 'Otley 'ill loike she were canterin' 'ome first in the bloody Durby. Jet haircraft ain't got nothin' on this one when oi stokes up th'ole foirebox." '

Buckinghamshire contains more footpaths than does any other county of comparable size. In the Chilterns they are especially numerous because the Hills were too steep and too sparsely populated to justify the building of a road over all the summits. Cottagers were content to follow footpaths, and they remained content until money and motors supplanted fitness and footwear. In 1937 scores of paths near my old home were used throughout the week by people from remote farms and hamlets; but in 1977 many of the rights-of-way had become overgrown, and some were impassable. A nineteenth-century American novelist, Nathaniel Hawthorne, set great store by England's footpaths. They wander, he said, 'from stile to stile, along hedges, and across fords, broad fields, and through wooded parks, leading you to little hamlets of thatched cottages, ancient, solitary farm-houses, streamlets, and all those quiet, secret, unexpected, yet strangely familiar features of the English scenery'.

Following those paths, you may within half-an-hour walk from Hampdenleaf Wood to Britain's most famous stately home, Chequers Court, so-called because it stands near the site of a department of King John's treasury, one of whose officials acquired the manor and with it a name, *de Scaccariis* or 'of the Exchequer'. Built in 1566, on the site of several earlier houses, the present Court is a handsome example of Tudor domestic architecture; redbricked, many-chimneyed, alone in a large park surrounded by wooded hills. At the beginning of the twentieth century the estate was bought by A. E. Lee, who ultimately received a barony. When Lloyd George became the first British premier without a country house at which to entertain distinguished visitors, Lee bequeathed the Court and part of its grounds for the use of British premiers in perpetuity. In 1972 the premier's official country seat was so delapidated that the American ambassador gave a large sum of money toward the cost of repairs. Many Britons approved the gift, but few expressed shame at needing to accept it.

Chequers Court is dominated by Coombe Hill, nearly nine hundred feet high, overlooking Oxfordshire, Berkshire, Bedfordshire, Gloucestershire, Hertfordshire, Northamptonshire, and Warwickshire. At the foot of Coombe Hill lies the Icknield Way, a prehistoric trade route from East Anglia to the Westcountry. Old people can remember the Icknield Way when it served as a drove road for cattle and sheep travelling between Wiltshire and Cambridgeshire. If you follow this green road over the Hills you will elude the suburbanisation that has marred the Chilterns. Between Bledlow and the foot of Swyncombe Downs the old drove road reveals the beauty which Pastor Moritz found when he, too, explored the Chilterns: 'one green hill after another, embellished with woodlands, meadows, hedges and villages ... there is not a spot where the eye does not long lovingly to dwell'. Amen, say I, who dwelt there lovingly for five-and-thirty years.

At the foot of the Chilterns a pleasant lane led to Longwick and the Vale of Aylesbury, a distance of scarcely two miles, yet long enough to offer a vivid example of scenic differences within a single county. Behind me stood a skyline of wooded hills; ahead lay a flat plain. Brick-and-flint cottages, typical of the chalkland, gave way to stone or to plain brick; cattle displaced corn; rivers and streams appeared, the products of earthquake and erosion. Few people nowadays are affected by this change of scene, but the Chiltern cottagers of fifty years ago were inclined to look down on the valesmen, physically as well as metaphorically. You may still hear an elderly hill-dweller speak of 'the folks living down there'. Sectors of the 'pleasant lane' had, I found, been 'improved' so that motorists could race to be first at the next bend. Having risked their lives, and other people's also, the winners reached Thame about one minute ahead of the losers.

Thame is a true country town with a very wide main street and a weekly market. The parish church was built of Headington stone by Robert Grosseteste. The Tudor Grammar School—now a business premises—educated three famous men: Mr Speaker Lenthall (to whom Charles I remarked that the birds had flown); Dr Fell (the allegedly unlikeable Dean of Christ Church, Oxford); and John Hampden (whom Lord Clarendon ranked with Cinna as a man 'with a head to contrive, and a tongue to persuade, and a hand to execute, any mischief'). Like every other English country town, Thame has been marred by serve-yourself-shops, by scores of traffic signs, by hordes of cars, by an eczema of anti-architecture, and by garages competing with one another across the street. Nevertheless, Thame at early morning in 1976 looked much the same as when I saw it at noon in 1922.

At Thame I faced a parting of the ways to Oxford. The quick way joined a motorway; the slow way (which was my way) led to Ickford, where the River Thame marks the border with Buckinghamshire. Not many years ago the men of Ickford inaugurated an annual tug-of-war with their Oxfordshire

41

neighbours across the water; a stirring and at times a sodden event, since neither side will yield until its tuggers have suffered a waist-deep immersion. Thus was added a new jewel to the diadem of English country customs: the Well-dressers at Tissington in Derbyshire, the Tar-branders at Allendale in Northumberland, the Flitchers at Dunmow in Essex, Hobby-horsers at Padstow in Cornwall, Cheese-rollers at Brockworth in Gloucestershire, Grovely processioners at Wishford in Worcestershire, Dolers at Tichborne in Hampshire, Pace-Eggers at Preston in Lancashire, and so many more that no man can name them all. Some of the customs long ago lost their *raison d'être* and became self-conscious; but others continue to endorse the wisdom of Hilaire Belloc when he said that men are 'nurtured sanely by a multiplicity of observed traditional things'.

From Ickford I walked to the riverside village of Waterstock, where the church stands beside the River Thame. This was Oxfordshire in a minor key, neither lofty, as in the Chilterns, nor commodious, as in the Cotswolds; yet placid, pastoral, pleasing. I am glad that I did choose the slow way to Oxford, because it soon afterwards suffered an 'improved road development'. Then, abruptly, the pleasure ended, for there is no gracious entry into Oxford. All the approaches are ugly, noisy, crowded. So, jostled by lorries and cars, I entered the most famous university in the world, and was immediately engulfed by what Joanna Canaan called 'an alien spirit, a spirit concerned with cinemas, hair-styles, and the Co-operative stores'.

What does one say of Oxford? Not, certainly, what was said to Pastor Moritz when he met the Vicar of Dorchester, with whom—since neither could speak the other's language fluently—he conversed in Latin. 'During the course of the conversation,' he wrote, 'we walked nearly into Oxford ... "Now," said the vicar, "you will soon see one of the most beautiful and superb cities not merely in England but in all Europe." ' What has happened to that 'beautiful and superb' city? It has been swamped and encircled by a car-crammed, shop-streaked, commercial hive, buzzing with ring roads and roundabouts and suburbs and factories. Once again, though, not all is lost, not yet, for there are certain hours and certain months when parts of the university may be seen as Erasmus saw them, as Cardinal Wolsey saw them, as Sir Thomas More, Sir Walter Raleigh, John Wesley, Adam Smith, Dr Johnson, Cardinal Newman, Shelley, Swinburne, and half the great men who governed England's greatness. Come, then, on a May morning, before the traffic has arrived; or in October, while the leaves are departing; or late on a snowy night, when you will hear what Horace Walpole heard two centuries ago: 'About a mile before I reached Oxford, all the bells tolled in different notes; the clocks of every college answered one another, and sounded forth (some in deeper, some in softer tones) that it was eleven at night . . .'. If he chooses the correct hour and the appropriate place, an Oxford man may still answer 'Yes' to Quiller-Couch's question:

Know you her secret none can utter,
Her of the Book, and tripled Crown?

And the 'Yes' will be justified because

Still on the spire the pigeons flutter,
Still by the gateway flits the gown,
Still in the street, from corbal and gutter,
Faces of stone peer down.

From time immemorial there has been a settlement at the ford where oxen crossed the Thames; and for more than seven hundred years the University of Oxford has remained *primus inter pares*, a fact that is acknowledged by Cambridge, whose oldest college, Peterhouse, was founded in 1284 'for studious scholars who shall in everything live together as students in the University of Cambridge according to the rule of scholars of Oxford . . .'.

Until the beginning of the twentieth century, Oxford was first and last a university; High Church, Tory, royalist; inclining rather to the Humanities than to science. True, the city had already suffered a severe attack of Victorian suburbs, but the residents thereof were either academics or some other class of person whose ethos did not clash with the university's. John Keble gave thanks that the citadel stood fast against Mammon:

The flood is all around thee, but thy towers as yet
Are safe; and, clear as by a summer's sea,
Pierce the calm morning mist, serene and free,
To point in silence heavenward.

By the end of the nineteenth century, however, industry and commerce had begun to throttle the city. William Morris witnessed the *fin-de-siècle*: 'When I remembered the contrast between the Oxford of today and the Oxford which I first saw thirty years ago, I wonder I can face the misery of visiting it . . .'. A later William Morris aggravated the process by building motorcar factories at Oxford.

The colleges vary in size, age, appearance, and repute. When I was an undergraduate, more than forty years ago, the two fashionable colleges were Magdalen and Christ Church, the latter being dubbed 'The House', an abbreviation of *Aedes Christi* or 'Christ's House', the name chosen by its founder, Cardinal Wolsey. Some colleges are linked with a famous school. Thus, Winchester has scholarships to its sister-foundation, New College; Merchant Taylors' has scholarships to its sister-foundation, St John's College. Other colleges maintain regional links; notably Jesus College (which attracts Welshmen), Exeter College (which attracts Westcountrymen), and Worcester College (which attracts men from the Midlands). The names and nicknames of colleges provide colloquial footnotes to history. New College, for instance, is the only Oxford college which at all times describes itself *qua* college; you may speak of Pembroke or of Trinity or of Keble, but never of New; always of New College. On formal occasions a comparable courtesy is extended to Queen's, which then becomes The Queen's College. Some of the other colleges cherish less august names, at any rate in conversation. St Edmund Hall is 'Teddy Hall'; University College is 'Univ'; and Brasenose College answers to its initials, 'BNC'. Likewise the styles of the heads of colleges vary, as between the Provost of Oriel, the Master of Balliol, the Warden of New College, the President of Magdalen, the Rector of Lincoln, and the Dean of Christ Church.

What is an Oxford college like? It is, in the first place, not quite like any other Oxford college, because each has its own history and customs. Oriel, which is among the larger and older colleges, is the one I know best. A brief account of it may therefore serve as a general introduction. Oriel was founded in 1326 by King Edward II at the suggestion of his almoner, Adam de Brome, who became the first Provost and also Vicar of St

Mary's Church, commonly though incorrectly called the University Church. The name 'Oriel' may have been taken from a house, *La Oriele*, which the King presented to his college. Oriel was rebuilt during the seventeenth century, and additions and alterations were made thereafter. The main entrance to the three quadrangles is a gatehouse with a fan-vaulted archway bearing the arms of the college and those of King James I. A room above the gatehouse has an oriel window, an oak fireplace, and a ceiling decorated with roses and *fleurs-de-lys*. The first quadrangle includes the hall, the chapel, and the buttery, which are reached via steps to a great porch crowned by statues of King Edward II and of King Charles I. The hall itself, fifty feet long, contains the finest hammerbeam roof in Oxford; at the far end, on a dais, stands the high table at which the dons dine; below it, lit by pink-shaded lamps, are refectory tables for the undergraduates; above, is a gallery for freshmen. I can still remember my first dinner in hall; the glowing lamps, gleaming silver, sleek young heads, bald old ones; the gowns and the laughter; on the panelled walls a portrait of Edward II enthroned, and around him the portraits of Sir Walter Raleigh and of centuries of peers, bishops, deans, statesmen, scholars, judges, poets. In that hall, on high occasions, they sing the Oriel Grace Cup Song: *Floreat Oriel in saecula saeculorum* (May Oriel prosper forever).

The second quadrangle contains the senior library and the senior common room, hung with portraits of Bishop Ken, Cardinal Newman, Dean Copleston, Lord Bryce, John Pusey, Matthew Arnold, James Anthony Froude, and other eminent Fellows. During the nineteenth century an Oriel Fellowship was Oxford's greatest academic distinction.

The third quadrangle is reached via the junior common room, which contains a portrait of my ancestor, saintly Sir Thomas More—Lord High Chancellor of England during the reign of Henry VIII—whose blessed memory commended me to the Provost of his old college. Parts of this quadrangle were rebuilt by the generosity of Cecil Rhodes, an Oriel graduate, who gave vast sums of money to the college, and endowed one-hundred-and-sixty Oxford scholarships, to be held by two students from every American State, and by three students from each of the eighteen British colonies; also fifteen scholarships for German students to be chosen by the Kaiser, William II. Rhodes House was built as a meeting place of Rhodes scholars.

For three memorable years, if he uses them aright, an Oxford undergraduate may move among scenes of noble example and unforgettable beauty. He may try for a rowing Blue, or be content to play cricket for his college. At the Oxford Union he may speak his own mind, and at the Oxford University Dramatic Society he may speak someone else's. He may share the companionship of his youthful peers, and the learning of some of the foremost scholars in the world. In my own day every Oxford undergraduate was required to be a passable Latinist, which meant that he had acquired some knowledge of the ancient world and of its literature and philosophy. All that has changed. In any event, the sum of human knowledge long ago exceeded any man's ability either to perceive or to comprehend it.

Of the difference between Oxonians past and Oxonians present I shall say no more than this; that some of the undergraduates now despise many of the ideals which Oxford has always preached and often practised. Such rebels might feel less itchy were they indoctrinated at an institution whose ethos was more to their liking. At the beginning of the twentieth century a university degree, and especially an Oxford degree, was a coveted distinction; today it is a commonplace. Yet Oxford still weaves her ancient spell. Wordsworth, a Cambridge man, confessed:

O ye spires of Oxford! domes and towers!
Gardens and groves! Your presence overpowers . . .

Another Cambridge man, Abraham Cowley, fell under the spell of Bodley's Library,

which well
Dost in the midst of Paradise arise,
Oxford, the Muses' Paradise!

From her own sons the university has received a paean of devotion. Matthew Arnold saw Oxford as the enemy of modern Philistines: 'home of lost causes, and forsaken beliefs, and unpopular names . . .'. Sir Arthur Quiller-Couch never forgot the first sight of his own Trinity College: 'The gardens lay below him; smooth turf flanked with a gay border of flowers, flanked on the other side with yews, and beyond the yews with an avenue of limes, and beyond these with tall elms . . . and over them the larks were singing. So this was Oxford; more beautiful than all his dreams!' Cardinal Newman wished to spend his whole life in the university:'There used,' he wrote, 'to be much snap-dragon on the walls of my freshman's rooms there, and I had for years taken it as an emblem of my perpetual residence even unto death in my university'. Oxford has weathered many storms. Therefore an Oxford man shares the faith of Robert Bridges:

Time shall against himself thy house uphold,
And build thy sanctuary from decay;
Children unborn shall be thy pride and stay.
May earth protect thee and thy sons be true . . .

From Oxford I doubled-back a few miles to Stanton St John, the *tun* or 'village' on stony ground, where one of the houses carried an inscription: 'The birthplace of John White, 1574–1648, fellow of New College, Oxford, and chief founder of the colony of Massachusetts in New England'. Stanton St John was the home of Milton's grandfather, an under-ranger of Shotover Forest, which in those years reached to the edge of Oxford. The poet sometimes visited his grandfather, and ultimately married the daughter of a neighbouring magistrate. Milton's nephew, Edward Philips, said that Milton had kept his wooing a secret: 'About Whitsuntide it was, or a little after, that he took a Journey into the Country; no body about him certainly knowing the Reason, or that it was any more than a Journey of Recreation; after a Month's stay, home he returns a Married man, that went out a Batchelor; his wife being Mary, the Eldest Daughter of Mr. Richard Powell, then a Justice of the Peace, of Forrest-hill, near Shotover in Oxfordshire . . .'.

For the next twenty miles I continued along a country road so familiar to me that I could remember many of the houses and some of the woods. The landscape was undramatic, peaceful, expansive. Southward the Chilterns stood like little mountains; all around, the soil assumed a tawny or oxidised tint. Drystone walls appeared. And every house was of stone.

Through Islip I went, a steep village beside the River Ray, with one or two shops and several thatched roofs. King Edward the Confessor was born at Islip, nearly a thousand years ago. The church, in fact, contains his portrait, inscribed with some words from his Will: 'I have given to Christ and St. Peter in Westminster ye little town of Islippe wherein I was born'. Turning from the sublime to the ridiculous, some people may wish to know about another Islip man, James Sadler, by trade a pastrycook, who became the first English aeronaut to survive his own folly. On 4 October 1784, having travelled from Oxford in a balloon, Sadler landed alive at Islip. Not since the invention of gunpowder had anyone set a precedent so fraught with death.

Death certainly confronted me a few miles beyond Islip, where the lane crossed a main road from Oxford to Birmingham. Having at last found a gap in the commercial cavalcade, I re-entered rural England, and continued along the lane while cows peered over hedges, sheep bleated from folds, and farmers went about their business of helping to feed England, a task which many townsfolk regard as the unskilled labour of those who are unfit for anything better. Yet agriculture produces the staff of life. Without factories a considerable number of people would survive and, in a quiet way, prosper; but without agriculture the entire population would die.

Flanked meanwhile by prime beef and rising corn, I entered Bletchingdon, another stone village. Bletchingdon Park, a relatively modern mansion, stands on the site of one of the few Cavalier strongholds which surrendered to the rebels without a struggle; whereafter its commander, Colonel Windebank, was court-martialled and shot *pour encourager les autres*. Bletchingdon has retained part of its green or common land, an obsolescent feature of the English countryside, though for centuries a hub of activity. Writing during the 1890s, Joseph Ashby cited the role of village greens: 'To this day every propagandist of a new religious idea, or a political creed, or a social reform has found his audience and perhaps some of his inspiration on those few yards of historic greensward'. In 1955 the Royal Commission on Common Land defined a village green as 'Any place which has been allotted for the exercise or recreation of the inhabitants of a parish or defined locality under the terms of any local Act or inclosure award ...'. But village greens never were mere playgrounds. On the contrary, they augmented a cottager's meagre income by allowing him to graze his pig or his cow gratis, and in certain places to dig peat or to collect firewood or to quarry stones. Despite the Enclosure Acts of the past two centuries, some villages maintain their common rights, as at Lamberhurst in Kent, where all the tenants of the manor may graze livestock on the green.

Soon after Bletchingdon the lane crossed another main road, and for the next half-mile was haunted by the drone of distant traffic. But sanity soon returned, guiding me to Glympton, a hamlet of stone houses beside the River Glyme. Cotswold stone is commonly called oolite (a compound of two Greek words, meaning 'egg' and 'stone'). If you examine oolite you will notice lumps of egg-shaped calcium carbonate, rather like a fish's roe. With that stone the local masons created some of the most beautiful houses in Britain. E. V. Lucas stated a fact when he said of the Cotswolds: 'the humblest barn is more beautifully ecclesiastic than the most pretentious of our latter-day churches, and cattle have sheds that surpass many cloisters'. The colour, texture, and durability of Cotswold stone varies with the district from which it is quarried. Some stones are grey; some are tinged with ochre; some glow like gold in the sun; all are handsome, dignified and literally a part of the landscape.

The lane through Glympton made a graceful double bend beside a stream and a green verge, thereafter climbing an avenue of trees, past the gateway to a manor house in a park containing a Norman church with a memorial to Thomas Tesdale, co-founder of Pembroke College, Oxford. Glympton is a place for all seasons. Spring kindles the candelabra on chestnut trees. Summer spreads the meadows with a cloth of golden buttercups. Autumn enters a brown study. Winter etches bare boughs.

Less than a mile beyond Glympton the lane joined yet another main road from Oxford to Birmingham, which I followed for about ten miles, through a rolling landscape of stone walls, tawny soil, wide skyline. The traffic, however, made it unwise to look at anything except the traffic. On the outskirts of Chipping Norton I escaped into a bylane, making a pilgrimage of grace to villages I had known for many years ... Ascott (a dozen

Cotswold houses sans church, or shop, or inn) . . . Barcheston (the smallest hamlet in the world, containing one house and a church whose tower leans like Pisa's) . . . Honington (where I used to put horses over the sticks) . . . and Shipston-on-Stour (a sheep town beside the River Stour). Progress had partly failed in its effort to spoil Shipston, for although the little square was a car park, and some of its shops had been replaced by chain stores, the redbrick George Hotel still buzzed with talk of corn, hunting, sheep, cabbage, kale, cricket, and the weather. The ancient watermill (now a hotel) still heard the music of its leat. Sheep Street still shone with comely houses that had been built for sixteenth-century wool merchants and seventeenth-century yeomen.

Before leaving Shipston, I visited the site of a single-line railway station which used to link the town with Moreton-in-

Romney Marsh, Kent

A wind from the sea sighs through these osiers, and in years gone by the marshland tracks echoed to the muffled tread of pack horses carrying contraband tobacco, brandy, sugar, spices, tea. Fierce battles were waged between smugglers and Excisemen. But nowadays all is peaceful, prosperous, prolific. Here graze the Romney Marsh sheep, famed for their fleece and meat. Here stretch infinite acres of roots and grain, a granary for the nation that must import most of its food. When John Davidson came this way he walked down to the sea:

Masts in the offing wagged their tops;
The swinging waves pealed on the shore;
The saffron beach, all diamond drops
And beads of surge, prolonged the roar.

In the heart of the Marsh the loudest sound is silence, composed and sung by birds and sheep and the distant sibilance of salt water rinsing shingle shores.

Marsh and Stratford-upon-Avon. Until the 1920s the Shipston train dawdled through meadows at a pace so leisurely that a friend of mine once outstripped it by riding his bicycle along the lanes. This idyllic byline resembled those which vexed Beatrix Potter in 1885: 'Four hours to go sixty miles,' she complained. 'When mushrooms are in season the guard gets out to pick them'. (On the Shipston line the fireman got out to open and shut the field-gates.) I pity the man who never travelled the English bylines in the days of steam. He has missed an adventure that will not recur. The smallest of those lines carried only a tank engine and two coaches, one of which contained a couple of first-class compartments so seldom occupied that to enter them was to raise the dust of ages from their white-lace antimacassars. As an undergraduate returning to north Buckinghamshire from Oxford, I sometimes travelled on a branch line. In exchange for a

A Kentish Oasthouse

'Kent,' wrote Jane Austen, 'has been called The Garden of England'. No other county possesses a finer display of neat villages, trim fields, spick-and-span houses, blossoming byways, and weathered oasthouses. On the eve of World War I England contained more than thirty-six thousand acres of hopfields, of which three-fifths were in Kent. Botanists classify the hop as *Humulus Lupulus*, a member of a nettle-stinging family. When ripe, the hop develops a cone-shaped head, and that is what the pickers gather. Machinery, however, has displaced most of the Cockneys who used to combine business with pleasure by hop-picking in Kent.

Vita Sackville-West, who spent most of her life in the county, confessed that not even she, a poet, could paint the portrait of a sunny spring day in Kent:

such days, such days so wealthy and so warm
As tempt the very busy bees to swarm,
Make the articulate poet silent . . .

silver threepenny piece, the Oxford porter stowed my trunk in the guard's van, unlocked a musty first class compartment, heaved my suitcase onto the rack, and—with his cap—dusted the blue plush seat. In lordly isolation I watched the fields fly by at thirty-five miles an hour, and presently heard the brakes grinding as we approached a station whereon stood a porter-cum-station-master-cum-signalman. Opening the window, I felt the sun on my face, and smelt the roses, for in those years every country station maintained its flowerbeds. On market days the small platform was crowded; but this was a Sunday, in an age when Sunday was a day of rest, not a time of travel. No one, therefore, alighted from the train, nor did anyone board it, except a vociferous hen-crate. While the guard tried to quieten those passengers, the porter chatted with the fireman, who was wiping his hands on a wisp of cotton waste. Many such conversations are imprinted on my memory.

'Suit the spuds, this 'ere weather,' says the porter.
'Oh ah,' nods the fireman.
''Eard about beer?'
'Beer?'
'It's going up.'
'Beer?'
'Another 'apenny. Ted brought the news with the twelve-ten out o' Euston.'

Before the fireman can curse the government, a breathless shout causes everyone to look up. A woman with a shopping basket is running across the fields.

'Late again,' sighs the porter. 'I said to 'er once, "If you was to start five minutes earlier, you might arrive in time to catch the train after the one you'd meant to".'

As the belated passenger flops into a compartment, the porter waves, the guard whistles, the engine replies. So, with leaking glands and gleaming pistons, the pageant proceeds to its next destination, watched en route by cottagers who regard their local train as more punctual than Big Ben.

Shipston, Ascott, Honington, Idlicote, Whatcote, Halford ... I found little change along those green lanes of Warwickshire. The few alterations were generally for the better; old thatch renewed, muddy yards paved, poverty outlawed, diseases conquered. Honington had lost its thatched post office-cum-village shop, but the loss occurred forty years ago, and was therefore unmourned by those who came after. The hamlet seemed as peaceful as ever, the Stour flowing dreamily under a small bridge in sight of Honington Hall, a seventeenth-century mansion alongside a Jacobean church with the tower of a thirteenth-century predecessor. Full marks to Sir Nikolaus Pevsner for hailing Honington as a 'Very pretty and tidy village'. Honington's white and flinty lanes were now metalled and grey. Their peace, however, prevailed; and on them and in the fields beside them were the mechanised heirs of the men whom John Drinkwater knew when he, too, lived in the Cotswolds:

> I see the little roads of twinkling white
> Busy with fieldward teams and market gear
> Of rosy men, cloth-gaitered, who can tell
> The many-minded changes of the year . . .

Brailes, a hilltop village near Shipston, was the birthplace of William Bishop, the first Roman Catholic prelate in post-Reformation England. A Roman church, built in 1728, stands beside the Tudor manor house in which he was born. Here I met the last practising wheelwright in Warwickshire, son of a man who lived at a time when, as Richard Jefferies observed, 'The wheelwright is perhaps the busiest man in the place . . .'. Having learned his craft during the 1930s, the Brailes wheelwright plied a brisk trade while World War II compelled farmers to maintain their wooden waggons. After the war, however, metal ousted timber. 'Today,' the wheelwright told me, 'I live by building new houses. My craft has become my hobby. I doubt whether I make or mend half-a-dozen wheels a year.'

By this time I had reached yet another example of scene-shifting within a few miles and in the same county, for the hilly landscape around Shipston-on-Stour differs from the level landscape around Stratford-upon-Avon, which Gerald Bullett described as 'the very heart of England, indeed of two Englands, the England of large mansions standing in well-wooded parks, and the England of green fields and of villages dingy with coal-dust and noisy looms'. Birmingham, in short, has stretched its tentacles to within a dozen miles of Shakespeare's birthplace, and not a great many more from the birthplace of Michael Drayton, author of *Poly-Olbion*, a verse guidebook to England, unique insofar as it contains thirty thousand lines, leavened with prose commentaries and short lyrics. Drayton was born in 1563 at the village of Powlsworth (now spelt Polesworth), where he became page to the squire, Sir Henry Goodman, 'the first cherisher of his muse'. Drayton, indeed, claimed the traditional *nascitur non fit*:

> For from my cradle (you must know that) I
> Was still inclin'd to noble Poesie . . .

A second patron was Sir Walter Ashton, 'my truly noble friend . . . which hath given me the best of those hours, whose leisure hath effected this which I now publish'. Few poets in those years were allowed to starve, unless by their own cussedness. Assured of leisure and a sufficient income, Drayton worked at his poem for fifteen years, all the while complaining that the Tudor wave-crest of Englishry had become a Stuart slough of Frenchiness: 'Some of the outlandish unnatural English (I know not how otherwise to express them) stick not to say there is nothing in this Island worth studying . . .'. Despite the cool reception given to the first eighteen chapters of his book, Drayton published another dozen, not without difficulty, as he confessed to his fellow-poet, Drummond of Hawthornden: 'I have done twelve books more . . . but it lieth by me, for the booksellers . . . are a company of base knaves, whom I scorn and kick at'. No doubt the booksellers uttered a *Tu quoque*.

Every educated Englishman ought to plough through the acres of Drayton's guidebook. When the going becomes too hard the reader may skip his way to more congenial pastures. Drayton's vast journey encompasses Cornwall, Devon, Somerset, Hampshire, Wiltshire, the Isle of Wight, Gloucestershire, and Wales, whence it goes via the Wrekin into Warwickshire,

> My native County, then, which so brave spirits hast bred,
> If there be any virtue yet remaining in thy earth,
> Or any good of thine breath'd'st into my birth,
> Accept it as thine own whilst now I sing of thee . . .

From Warwickshire the route leads through Evesham to the Cotswolds, Oxford, Surrey, Sussex, Kent; at which point the breathless reader is carried northward once again, this time to Lincolnshire, Nottinghamshire, Lancashire, the Isle of Man, Yorkshire, Northumberland, and Westmorland.

Did Drayton really follow the poem's footsteps? Some he may have followed; others he travelled from hearsay, as when he remarked that the Foss Way stretches

from Michael's utmost Mount
To Caithness, which the furth'st of Scotland we account.

Despite some false topography, *Poly-Olbion* paints a vivid portrait of England as it appeared to a Tudor antiquarian whose fame prospered better in death than in life, for they buried him under the north wall of the nave in Westminster Abbey, with an epitaph by his friend, Ben Jonson. A later generation placed his bust in Poets' Corner. In 1974, having mislaid my second volume of *Poly-Olbion*, I obtained a copy from the public library. Curious to discover when it had last been borrowed, I glanced at the fly-leaf, which stated that the book must be returned not later than 24 October 1910.

From thinking on Drayton I was led to remember Shakespeare, born—as John Masefield put it—'in a twofold district of hill and valley, where country life was at its best and the beauty of England at its bravest'. The district is indeed a panorama of little hills and shallow valleys, of thatched cottages and timbered houses, of oaks and elms rising like lonely rocks from a sea of green pastures; and in it you can box the compass by naming the places that are associated with Shakespeare. At Wilmcote is his mother's old home, a black-and-white farmhouse. At Shottery is his wife's old home, Anne Hathaway's Cottage, a large house with twelve rooms (restored after arson in 1969). At Aston Cantlow is the church in which his parents are said to have been married (we know that the wedding took place in 1557, but the church registers did not begin until 1561). At Kineton his eldest daughter, Susanna Hall, entertained Charles I on the eve of the Battle of Edgehill. At Billesley his grand-daughter, Elizabeth Nash, married John Barnard. Some of the associations are unverified and probably spurious. Thus, a certain John Jordan announced that Shakespeare was once discovered drunk and incapable at the village of Bidford; but the allegation is impugned by the fact that Jordan, a semi-literate wheelwright, died two centuries after Shakespeare was born. Then there is Charlecote Park, a Tudor mansion, still owned by descendants of the Sir Thomas Lucy who held it in Shakespeare's day. Tradition says that young William poached a deer from the Park; that he was punished for it; that he then composed a libel on Sir Thomas, one stanza of which he pinned Lutherwise on the gatehouse door; that he soon afterwards lost his nerve, fled to London, earned a living as what we would now call a horse-park attendant outside a theatre; and that he ultimately revenged himself by parodying Sir Thomas Lucy as Sir Robert Shallow, whose coat was infested with 'luces' or lice. In Shakespeare's day, however, the Charlecote estate was not formally encamped, and deer-stalkers were therefore not breaching the laws of property. In any event, the verifiable associations are numerous enough to occupy a long pilgrimage. At Barton-on-the-Heath lived Shakespeare's cousins, the Lamberts; as also did one of the characters from *The Taming of the Shrew*: 'Am I not Christopher Sly, old Sly's son of Burtonheath, by birth a pedlar, by education a cardmaker, by transmutation a bear-herd, and now by present profession a tinker?'. At Hampton-in-Arden, or very near it, Shakespeare set the heart of *As You Like It*: 'They say he is already in the forest of Arden, and many a merry man with him; and there they live like the old Robin Hood of England . . . and fleet the time carelessly, as they did in the golden world'. Shakespeare's father lived for many years at Snitterfield, where a seat near the war memorial bears an inscription: 'The noble expanse visible from this spot was Shakespeare's favourite countryside. The men whose names are inscribed on the neighbouring monument gave their lives for that England which never did nor ever shall lie at the proud foot of a conqueror'.

But, of course, the most powerful magnet is Stratford-upon-Avon, a hotch-potch of traffic, factories, suburbs, supermarkets. The wellknown Shakespeare director, Bridges-Adams, cited Stratford's commercialism as 'the spiritual unloveliness which flourishes when people are content to make profits out of a great reputation'. Pastor Moritz said much the same thing in 1782: 'Shakespeare's chair, on which he used to sit in front of his door, is already so hacked away that barely anything of a chair is to be seen. For everyone who passes through this town cuts himself a chip off it to carry away as a relic'. The Pastor himself was not without sin: 'I cut off my bit,' he confessed, 'but it was too small and I have lost it'. In 1909 Sir Arthur Quiller-Couch's *True Tilda* uttered its own protest: 'You can't get away from Shakespeare here. If you buy a bottle of beer, he's on the label; and if you want a tobacco-jar, they'll sell you his head and shoulders in china . . .'. How, then, did Stratford prosper in the years before Shakespeare helped to subsidise it? Stratford prospered as a market town with an inland harbour for vessels plying on the River Avon.

According to local tradition, Shakespeare was born at a half-timbered house which in 1670 passed to his great-nephew, Thomas Hart, and thereafter remained with the Hart family until 1806, when it was sold for £210; part of it being then a tavern, and part a butcher's shop. Pastor Moritz found the place 'one of the poorest, worst preserved, and most unseemly houses in Stratford . . . In this house lived an old couple who make a living by showing it to strangers'. In 1891 the Trustees and Guardians of Shakespeare's Birthplace began the task of restoration and preservation.

Unlike many other artists, Shakespeare was neither a spendthrift nor a disrespector of persons. At the age of thirty-three, while still an active dramatist, he prepared for his retirement by purchasing a sizeable house at Stratford, costing £60, which he renovated and renamed as New Place. The most eminent visitor to New Place was Queen Henrietta Maria, who stayed there for three nights as the guest of Shakespeare's daughter, Susanna. In 1753 the house was sold to the Rev Francis Gastrell, a Philistine from Cheshire, who soon afterwards demolished it. Among the town's other notable buildings are the half-timbered and red-roofed Grammar School (where Shakespeare learned some Latin and Greek); Harvard House, built in 1596 by Thomas Rogers (his daughter, Mrs Harvard, gave birth in 1605 to John Harvard, who bequeathed £779 17s 2d for the founding of Harvard University); and a twentieth-century theatre (which from a distance resembles an obsolete power house).

What, finally, of Shakespeare himself? Of no other great Englishman do we know so little; nor has any other been the subject of so many books. Even his birthday is doubtful. Tradition gives it as St George's Day, 23 April 1564; but the parish register, while confirming that the baptism took place on 26 April, does not state the date of birth; it merely names the infant as *Gulielmus filius Johannes Shakespere* or 'William, son of John Shakespere'. His father was a glover, a curer of hides, and the town ale-taster, who proved the flexibility of English society by acquiring a coat-of-arms with the motto *Non Sanz Droict* or 'Not Without Right'. Shakespeare's mother, Mary Arden, was a yeoman's daughter. Married when he was eighteen—six months before the birth of his first child—Shakespeare begat one son and two daughters. Disliking Benedik's role of married man, he migrated to London, became an actor, wrote some plays, retired to Stratford, and there died, supposedly on his fifty-second birthday, St George's Day 1616. He was buried as 'Will Shakespeare, gent', in the chancel of the Church of the Holy Trinity, which he had served as lay rector by virtue of his status as a tithe-owner.

What is the nature of Shakespeare's achievement? Some people are content to describe him as 'the greatest Englishman who has ever lived'. International scholarship certainly ranks him as one of the world's finest dramatists and perhaps the supreme poet. However, there is no reason to regard him as a great personality nor as a great man of action. He lives in his art, and he foresaw that fact:

> So long as men can breathe, or eyes can see,
> So long lives this, and this gives life to thee.

Ben Jonson, his friend and fellow-dramatist, viewed him with envious admiration. In 1619, three years after Shakespeare's death, Jonson visited William Drummond, who took notes of their conversation: 'Shakespeare,' declared Jonson, 'wanted Arte'. Twenty years later, in *Discoveries*, Jonson recorded some other impressions of his friend: 'He was (indeed) honest, and of an open, and free nature; had an excellent *Phantasie*; brave

notions, and gentle expressions: wherein he flow'd with that
facility that sometime it was necessary he should be stop'd'.
That Shakespeare occasionally talked too much is probably true;
that he 'wanted Arte' is manifestly false. In the end, however,
Jonson paid to Shakespeare a tribute such as few poets have had
the good fortune to receive, or the magnaminity to bestow: 'To
the memory of my beloved The Author Mr William Shakespeare
And what he hath left us'.

What *has* he left us? Beyond doubt, the greatest plays yet
written in our language, and the deepest psychological insight
until Freud compiled a technical glossary. But Shakespeare was
not flawless. Like Homer, he sometimes nodded, preferring
rather to borrow than to invent his plots. For the sake of the box
office he sometimes descended to the level of the gallery, which in
his day stood on the ground floor ('the groundlings').
Nevertheless, only one other artist, Beethoven, has travelled
further 'through strange seas of thought, alone'. Only one other
work of art, the Authorised Version of the Bible, has exerted a
deeper influence throughout the English-speaking world. On the
English themselves his impact is incalculable. Wordsworth used
it as a rallying cry for the entire kingdom:

> We must be free or die, who speak the tongue
> That Shakespeare spake.

Robert Bridges said of him, that God had

> Doubled his whole creation, making thee . . .

Matthew Arnold set him, not above criticism, but beyond the
range of any other human being:

> Others abide our question. Thou art free;
> We ask and ask. Thou smilest and art still
> Out-topping knowledge.

Some people assert that Shakespeare was a Christian; others,
that he was an atheist. Like the Bible itself, he can be quoted to
support rival hypotheses. But one thing is certain; his plays are
profoundly moral. *Othello* is a sermon against jealousy; *King Lear*,
a sermon against ingratitude; *Macbeth*, a sermon against
ambition; *Hamlet*, a sermon against indecision. It is as though

Shakespeare had anticipated D. H. Lawrence's *credo*: 'All art is moral' ... but a morality preached with such skill that the audience never feels itself to be a congregation. Without distorting the common usage of language, or needing to explain himself by means of notes, Shakespeare devised what may justly be called a new style of poetry, whose propositions and evocations are immediately comprehensible to an educated reader, according to his intellectual and imaginative equipment. Consider *The Phoenix and the Turtle*, a poem of eighteen brief stanzas, describing the fusion through fission of two affections:

Reason, in itself confounded,
Saw division grow together,
To themselves yet either neither,
Simple were so well compounded ...

There indeed the pinnacle of human thought explores the depths; brevity encompasses totality; and style outdates the fashion.

Shakespeare lived at a time when the genius or spirit of the English people stood at its zenith. Not even the Victorians achieved so swift and fine a flowering of the arts. Gentle and simple, rich and poor, young and old, town and country ... every Elizabethan shared the awareness of riding high. Their buildings perpetuate that fact. Their poetry sings it. Their seamanship flaunts it. Their enemies acknowledge it. 'If,' wrote Paul Hertzn, 'they see a foreigner very well made, or particularly handsome, they say, "It is a pity he is not an Englishman.".' Such arrogance is one of the reasons why the Elizabethans did ride high. Shakespeare himself believed that only England can defeat England:

This England never did nor ever shall,
Lie at the proud foot of a conquerer,
But when it first did help to wound itself.

Wandering through rural Warwickshire, I observed that many of the older people felt powerless either to rebuild the past or to control the present. 'What,' they asked, 'has *happened* to England? Why must we always copy French ways, or German ways, or American ways? Why don't they copy *us* for a change?

Let 'em turn their litres into pints, and start driving on the English side of the road, Why don't we send a battleship there, and put a stop to all the fighting?' This swift reversal of roles did not disturb the young, who seemed scarcely conscious that it had occurred. Some of them were content to attend drug festivals or to brandish puerile placards, each youth wearing the soiled and bi-sexual uniform of nonconformity. Others—conscious that they must mould the future—shouldered their task with a blend of bewildered idealism and commercial acumen, trusting that those who had once ruled the waves would manage to survive as a nation of shopkeepers.

4 EAST ANGLIA

East Anglia includes Cambridgeshire, Huntingdonshire, Norfolk, and Suffolk; to which some people might add the north-eastern tip of Bedfordshire and the northernmost part of Essex. This cold yet fertile region was named after the *East Angle* or 'East Angles', who settled among what are now the counties of Norfolk and Suffolk, whence they moved inland via Northamptonshire, a region whose broad acres and splendid churches caused it to be known as 'the county of spires and squires'. One family of Northamptonshire squires achieved international fame, for in 1560 Laurence Washington built a two-storey manor house at Sulgrave, now a museum, much visited by compatriots of Laurence's descendant, Colonel George Washington, first President of the United States of America. Despite some outbreaks of industry, Northamptonshire remains primarily an agricultural county, whose landowners tend their estates as zealously as they chase the foxes thereon. The grassland glistens; the hedges and coverts are made-to-measure for pink-coated riders; the stone manor houses wear a lordly look. At Canons Ashby, for example, the Dryden family in 1551 built a house on the site of an eleventh-century abbey. Thither came several famous writers, including Edmund Spenser, John Dryden, and Samuel Richardson, author of *Sir Charles Grandison* (in which the first section is headed 'Ashby-Canons').

From Ashby Canons I made for Northampton, which Defoe rated as 'the handsomest and best built town in all this part of England'. But that was two centuries ago. Today the few remaining Georgian houses are lost among an assortment of Victorian and Atomic prosperity. Northampton makes shoes. In the thick of it I got lost, so inadequate were the sign posts to an intricate route through a labyrinth of side streets. When I recovered, half-an-hour later, I found myself at Kettering; and there also I got lost. Kettering makes everything, or ought to, if traffic and factories are a reliable guide. Driving wearily through an industrial landscape I relieved the lorry-laden tedium by remembering the many pleasant places which, although they lay within easy reach of my route, must abide beyond it: Oundle, for example, that handsome little town, where almost every building is good to look at and comfortable to occupy. In 1910 or thereabouts a certain Wakeling Dry wrote: 'the speculative builder has happily not yet laid his fell grasp on Oundle'. The same may be said in 1977, chiefly because of Oundle School, founded in 1566 by a local grocer, William Laxton. Among the many beautiful buildings are an Early English church; the seventeenth-century Talbot Inn; and the elder of two almshouses, known as Latham's Hospital, a miniature replica of an Oxford college. Only the lorries disturb the air of gay tranquility that pervades this small town with a famous school presiding *in loco parentis*. You will find a comparable dignity and self-preservation at Sedbergh in Yorkshire, at Holt in Norfolk, at St Bees in Cumberland, at Monkton Combe in Somerset, and Uppingham in Rutland.

From Oundle I once walked into Fotheringhay, a hamlet of quietude in an oasis of peace. There, beside the meditative River Nene, stood a church, foreshortened by the fire that had damaged it four centuries ago. Only a green mound marked the site of the castle where Mary Queen of Scots was tried and executed. Having harangued her judges, that troubled and troublesome Queen walked calmly 'into the hall within the said castle of ffotherghaie . . . with an unapauled countenance stept up to the scaffold in the said hall . . . and there made her death'. But we have wandered, and are co-opting those places which we ought not to have co-opted.

On the road to Huntingdon I sighted the western edge of the Fens. More precisely, I saw wide skies above flat fields, and over them the birds that haunt damp places. Huntingdon in 1086 was called *Huntedun*, meaning either 'Hunta's Hill' or 'Huntsman's Hill'. Hunta, if he ever existed, was certainly a local chief; but of the huntsman and his quarry we know nothing. The county town is as agreeable as when Cobbett admired it: 'Huntingdon,' he wrote, 'I like exceedingly ... it is one of those clean, unstenched, unconfined places that tend to lengthen life and make it happy ...'. The traffic, although brisk, seldom becomes unbearable. Indeed, there are moments when Huntingdon is *quiet*. The former Grammar School educated Samuel Pepys and Oliver Cromwell. Pepys's family home is a fifteenth-century farmhouse in the neighbouring village of Brampton, where (they say) the diarist buried his money when the Dutch seemed likely to invade England. In the same neighbourhood stands the county's stateliest home, Hinchingbrooke House, Built by Sir Richard Cromwell, grandfather of Oliver Cromwell, a figure unique in our history because he plotted to create and then contrived to destroy the only English Republic. Cromwell is a notable example of the rebel who becomes more tyrannical than the regime which he has supplanted. Thus, although the murder of Charles I was neither necessary nor desirable, Cromwell personally threatened any of the regicides who hesitated to sign the illegal death warrant. That done, he led his troops into the House of Commons; caused the Speaker to be dragged from his chair; and then announced that he would hang anyone who called him a usurper. When a group of Salisbury shopkeepers protested, they were transported as slaves to Barbados, without the formality of a trial. The Press was muzzled; the Church and the Prayer Book were outlawed; and people who kissed under the mistletoe were liable to be whipped, fined, or imprisoned. Cromwell assumed a quasi-regal title, His Highness The Lord Protector; and he packed and threatened and disregarded Parliament in a manner which no other man has dared to do. Even the rebels rebelled. Francis White, a member of the Army Council, declared 'there is now no visible authority in the kingdom, but the power of the sword'. Cromwell, in fact, was so hated that the Venetian ambassador reported: 'Cromwell never slept in the same room, but frequently changed his bed, for fear of mines'.

Faced by widespread unrest, the Protector divided the kingdom into eleven zones, each commanded by a Major General; but martial law proved so disastrous that he was forced to recall Parliament. Before voting took place, however, he ordered his Major Generals to rig the elections by intimidating the electors. Writing from Cheshire, Major General Tobias assured Cromwell: 'I have taken the best course possible ... to procure the election'. Although one-third of the new members were Cromwell's toadies, nearly one hundred others were forcibly prevented from taking their seats. Cromwell now graciously consented to declare himself His Majesty King Oliver the First. The Genoese ambassador reported: 'Cromwell goes on with his plan ... to accept the Throne'. On 6 May 1657 he did accept, but soon afterwards changed his mind, in deference to the republican junta on whose backs he had climbed to power. Of his massacres in Ireland it is enough to observe that the Irish have never forgotten them. Meanwhile, he governed as an absolute military dictator. The Venetian envoy wrote: 'Cromwell is more powerful than all the Kings that have ever been in England'. But power did not bring prosperity; at Cromwell's death the national debt nearly exceeded the national revenue. When at last Charles II returned to his own he was received with an enthusiasm which surprised even the worldly Pepys: 'The shouting and joy expressed by all is past imagination ... a day of rejoicing for our redemption'.

A century after Cromwell's death, William Marshall collected material for a survey of English agriculture. Cambridgeshire, he said, was the worst-farmed county in England; nor did Huntingdonshire fare much better: 'The disgraceful state in which some of those lands were suffered to remain ...'. Today those lands are among the most fertile in Britain, intensively cultivated for wheat, barley, vegetables, hay, flowers, meat.

On the road from Huntingdon to Cambridge I met a mild version of the east wind that had greeted Celia Fiennes on her way from Huntingdon to Stilton: 'Sudden winds,' she shivered, 'that will rise like Hurricanes'. Defoe, too, felt the blast, and cursed the entire East Anglian climate: 'a horrid air for a stranger to breathe'. Horrid or not, the air once nurtured the springtime of Erasmus, Spenser, Milton, Newton, Pitt, Wordsworth, Tennyson, Darwin, Keynes, Russell, and countless other members of the University of Cambridge.

Wiser than Oxford, Cambridge keeps its ancient Gown somewhat apart from its modern Town, thereby creating what a twentieth-century Cambridge don, C. R. Benstead, described as 'a core of antiquity surrounded by modern expansion'. An ancient rivalry exists between our two great universities, symbolised by the shades of blue that were adopted during the early years of the Boat Race, when a member of the Cambridge crew, an Old Etonian, wore the light blue of his school; to which Oxford replied with a hue that needs less laundering. The rivalry itself is healthy and nowadays friendly. In 1598, by contrast, the feud was so bitter that Thomas Bastard exhorted the enemies to sign a truce:

> Ye famous sister Universities,
> Oxford and Cambridge, whence proceeds your hate?
> Why strive ye sisters for antiquity?
> Cannot your present honour you suffice?

Berkshire Ridgeway

Wessex contains several green roads whose origins can be told in a single stanza:

> Nomads first made
> This highway for trade
> While they roamed in search of new grass to graze;
> Their herds were a spade
> Through heather and glade
> In years that are hidden behind a haze.

Then came the barefoot Celts – Britain's earliest commercial travellers – shouldering their imports and exports. Some of the roads spanned England from coast to coast. Others led to religious shrines such as Stonehenge. All followed a lonely course over the hills and faraway. Now they are trodden only by farmfolk and a few pilgrims in search of peace.

This ridgeway reaches its zenith near Inkpen, where it passes a gallows astride a bare hill from which the Cotswolds are visible. On these prehistoric roads you may wander for hours without meeting a soul.

Nevertheless, a precedence does exist, and it belongs to Oxford. Said John Selden, the Caroline jurist: 'The best argument why Oxford should have precedence of Cambridge is the Act of Parliament, by which Oxford is made a body ... Besides, Oxford has the best monuments to show'. Selden's reference to architecture may sound like special pleading, yet his opinion was shared by John Lyly, a graduate of both places, whose *Euphues and his England* affirmed: 'There are also in this Island two famous Universities, the one Oxford, the other Cambridge ... excelling all the Universities of Christendom ... Colleges in Oxenford are much more stately for the building, and Cambridge much much sumptuous for the town ...'. Whereas Oxford has for centuries been Tory, Royalist, High Church, and Classical, Cambridge was ever a somewhat dissenting place, latterly inclined rather to Science than to the

Near Alton, Hampshire
Adze, froe, pick, brace, bittle, bille . . . a hurdle-maker uses those ancient tools whenever he makes a hurdle for penning animals or enclosing a plot of land. He uses the same tools when making walking sticks, scout poles, hop poles, and clothes pegs.

In wintertime the hurdler fells his timber and then chops it into various lengths, tying each bundle with a hazel 'ribbon'. For hop poles he prefers chestnut; for hurdles he prefers willow and ash. In springtime he splits and weaves his wood, using thick rods for the wattle uprights. Weaving is done around a hurdle-mould, seven feet long, with ten equidistant holes arranged in a slight curve. Into these holes the wattle uprights are fixed. Then the strips of wood are woven in and out of the staves. Much has been written about the mystique of craftsmanship, but no craft can survive unless it adopts new devices to meet new demands.

Humanities. So long ago as 1850 the university invited a literary don to compile a primer that would teach scientists how to write their own language.

Like Oxford, the medieval University of Cambridge acquired many privileges, and from the townsfolk much enmity. Thus, the Proctors or maintainers of university discipline who patrolled the streets on horseback (their constables still on occasion carry a symbolic horse-cloak). The Proctors licensed the ale houses, controlled the markets, and measured the imports of coal and grain (one of the Junior Proctor's constables still on occasion carries a butter-measure that was used when that commodity was sold by the yard). The feud between Town and Gown took an unconscionable time to die. In 1848 an undergraduate informed his mother: 'there is a Town and Gown row at present raging every night in the streets'. Members of the university, he added, were in danger of having their heads 'broken by the vulgar rabble. It is a serious thing when a quarrel of this kind commences; it may require weeks to end it. The Proctors have a sad time . . .'. Although the Award Act of 1856 abolished many of the university privileges, the Master of Trinity Hall may still grant marriage licences to anyone of his choice.

The oldest Cambridge college is Peterhouse. Which college is the most illustrious? Being a stranger to Cambridge, I shall merely report that some people award the prize to the College of the Holy and Undivided Trinity, an amalgam of two earlier houses, Michaelhouse and King's Hall, wherewith Henry VIII aspired to outshine all the other colleges. Trinity is in every sense a royal foundation. During the eighteenth century, under the Mastership of Richard Bentley, a Yorkshire stonemason's son, it became in many ways a law unto itself. As steward of a royal house, the Master of Trinity enjoyed the right to educate a quota of the Royal Princes, to lodge the Judges of Assize, and to entertain the Sovereign on his or her visits to the university. When William Whewell was Master of Trinity he invited Queen Victoria to rest awhile at his house; to which she replied: 'At *my* house, Mr. Whewell'.

Some people say that the most illustrious Cambridge college is King's, another royal foundation. It was in 1441, eleven months after he had established Eton College, that Henry VI, being then

nineteen years old, founded The King's College of Our Lady and
St Nicholas, which ever after owed its eminence to the links with
Eton, for membership of the college was at one time confined to
Etonians, the so-called Kingsmen, who could graduate without
passing an examination. Henry VI, at all events, ensured that
the college chapel should resemble a cathedral. His plan shows a
church forty feet wide, ninety feet high, and two hundred-and-
eighty feet long. Supervised by an East Anglian mason, Ronald
of Ely, limestone from the college estates in Yorkshire was
shipped via King's Lynn and thence up-river to Cambridge. The
choir of King's College Chapel is famous throughout the world,
especially for its annual festival of Christmas carols. But fame is
not a prerogative of any one college. Every ancient foundation
answers to its own resounding roll-call, and every alumnus owes
as much allegiance to his college as to his university. Cambridge
has received many memorable and unsolicited testimonials from
her sons. Among the more recent is the thanksgiving from Lance
Sieveking, a pioneer of radio drama: 'Cambridge,' he wrote, 'is
not only the vibrations of the youth of today, but the emanated
emotions of thousands of yesterdays; of the love, happiness, and
gratitude of those who have had in this place the richest
experience of their lives'.

Were I asked to name the symbol of that rich experience I
would choose those college gardens which slope to the river,
creating a waterscape unique in Britain, known to generations of
Cambridge men as 'The Backs'. Only a painter can adequately
portray the beauty of that scene, and only when it is not crowded
with people. If, therefore, you would savour the best of this
famous university, you must, as at Oxford, choose your season
and your hour. Come early, when the daffodils sway like
anchored suns beside the Cam; when bare and budding
branches reveal venerable vistas; when silence is more eloquent
than words.

From Cambridge I travelled north-east through Fenland, a
region once so barren, yet now so fertile, that its present
appearance would have astounded the medieval chronicler who
wrote of 'The great marsh in which lies the Isle of Ely'. Nowhere
else in Britain will you find a more impressive example of what
we call 'man's conquest of Nature', though it would be less

arrogant to say that Nature in Fenland has been domesticated to suit man's needs. In the remote past, about thirty thousand years ago, the region was a wilderness of birch and pine which, when the climate grew less cold, gave way to elm and oak. About the year 5,500 BC the rains increased, causing elders to rise beside the rivers. Then came more water, choking the woodlands with sedge and reed. Then again the climate relented, and again the woodlands arose. Suddenly the sea poured in, perhaps through a rupture of the coastal bar dividing Fenland from the Wash. As a result, the peat acquired a layer of greasy clay, in which the Bronze Age folk left some of their artefacts. During the Roman occupation the sea once more poured in, but this time it was met by the foremost civil engineers of the ancient world, who dug several canals to serve partly as drains and partly as inland waterways carrying Nottinghamshire coal to the sparsely wooded Fens. More than a thousand years elapsed before those Roman canals were repaired and extended, and even then the work was planned by a Dutchman, Cornelius Vermuyden, who constructed a canal from Earith to Denver Sluice, a distance of twenty-one miles. For his achievements in Fenland and the Yorkshire marshes, Vermuyden was knighted by Charles I. During the next three centuries an army of windmills and steam-pumps fought a perennial battle against floods, to create a new and fruitful region, eighty miles long and thirty miles wide. The chief victims of that battle were the Fensmen themselves, who gradually lost their amphibious economy of fishing, wild-fowling, and farming. Parts of Fenland are so flat that a hayrick looms like a church tower; so thinly wooded that six trees compose a copse; so free from industrial pollution that, as Charles Kingsley remarked, 'the arch of the heavens spread more ample than elsewhere . . . such cloudbanks, such sunrises, such sunsets, as can be seen nowhere else within these isles'. Lacking a plentiful supply of local timber and stone, Fenland never achieved a domestic architecture comparable with those of Gloucestershire or of Shropshire. Most of the present Fenland homesteads were built during the nineteenth century, of yellowish brick. Against them, however, stand a number of eighteenth-century houses, notably at Spalding and Wisbech. The typical Fenland road stretches like a causeway across an ocean of crops. In some places the barley creeps hip-high to within a few feet of a farmhouse door; in other places the dykes run like the ridges of an infinite furrow which in frosty weather provide the rinks that enabled Fensmen to become Britain's finest skaters. When I lived in the Fens during World War I it was not unusual to see housewives skating to the village shop.

In these parts, we agreed, a hayrick looms like a church tower. How much more dramatic, therefore, is the tower of Ely Cathedral, seen from afar. Founded in 1087, on the site of a seventh-century Benedictine Abbey, the cathedral out-tops all other buildings for miles around. During the Middle Ages it must have loomed like a fortress in a Sargasso swamp. In 1332—when the weight of masonry proved too great for the marshy foundation—the central tower collapsed and was replaced by Adam de Walsingham's lantern-roof, a glorious vision, unique in English architecture. Among the city's secular antiquities are a fourteenth-century Treasury; a fifteenth-century White Hart Inn; and Henry VIII's Grammar School, a successor to the Benedictine academy that educated Islip's King Edward the Confessor. Ely was called *Eleq* or 'eel island' because those creatures were so plentiful that they became a form of currency. The Ely monks, in fact, paid four thousand eels each year to Barnack quarry for the stone with which they built their cathedral (whence the saying 'Ely Cathedral was built of eels'). Today the city lies in Cambridgeshire; but Hereward the Wake knew it as an Island in a marsh, exercising a degree of autonomy comparable with the soke or local jurisdiction of Peterborough.

Fenland is the only region of Britain where you can travel by drain, as, for example, along the Sixteen Foot Drain, the engineers' name for a road northward from Chatteris. My own road passed within sight of the River Ouse and two dykes, the Old and the New Bedford Rivers. At Littleport I entered the land of my paternal grandmother, who used to tell me tales about the Littleport witches, one of whom, a seventeenth-century Anne Symes, was arrested for bewitching to death the vicar's daughter. However, I passed through Littleport unscathed, despite a railwayman who told me that his aunt drank potions to ward off the evil eye.

About four miles beyond Littleport Bridge I reached Norfolk, which Domesday Book called *Nordfolc*, to distinguish it from *Sudfolc* or 'the land of the south folk'. Now some county borders are slow to unfold a change of scene. On Exmoor, for example, if you cross from Devonshire into Somerset, you may travel nearly twenty miles without detecting any conspicuous change in scenery, climate, architecture, occupations, dialect; but within a few miles from Littleport Bridge the county border reveals many changes. Yellowish brick gives way to red brick and sometimes to brick-and-flint. Trees multiply, and become woods. Flat ploughland yields to undulant pastures. The east wind loses something of its sting. And instead of sighting your destination ten miles away, you find a skyline rippled with little hills. J. W. M. Turner called the landscape 'elegant pastoral'.

Norfolk itself ranks next in size after Yorkshire, Devonshire, and Lincolnshire. Few other English counties offer a more varied landscape . . . the Broads, the Breckland heaths, several fenlike zones, large areas of arable and pasture, innumerable small woods, nearly one hundred miles of coastline, and the finest parish churches in Britain.

Despite the heavy traffic, I found that Swaffham was still a country town of redbrick houses, market buildings, and some lime trees leading to a church where they buried Cromwell's grandmother, Catherine Steward, from whose daughter he inherited a considerable addition to his own estates. Swaffham's role as a market town is confirmed by an eighteenth-century rotunda or market cross, a gift from Horace Walpole, fourth Earl of Oxford.

Three miles beyond Swaffham a narrow lane led to Castle Acre, the *aecer* or 'field' on which a castle was built by the Conqueror's son-in-law, William Warenne, Earl of Surrey. This small village stands astride the Peddars Way, a Roman road from Ixworth in Suffolk to Holme-next-the-Sea in Norfolk. I once walked Peddars Way, piecing it together from sectors of modern tarmac and ancient turf. Castle Acre, therefore, offers a cross-section of English history, beginning with the flints that were chipped into tools by prehistoric hunters; then the coming of the Romans; then a medieval castle and priory; then the work of builders from the eighteenth to the twentieth centuries; and, over all, aircraft and television aerials.

On this journey I arrived via a steep lane, passing under the castle's arched gatehouse and then crossing a village green flanked by the cottages and trees that make Castle Acre seem always fresh and everlastingly old. Only the Victoria and Albert Inn looks misplaced, and only from the outside, because on my first arrival, at teatime during summer, I was received hospitably. Within five minutes a table had been set in the bar, and soon afterwards laden with boiled eggs, brown bread, fruit cake, sweet tea. Through an open window came the scent of new-mown grass, and the song of a blackbird. The rest was silence until six children began to romp on the green. One day, I thought, those children may look back in gratitude when they compare their own upbringing with the lot of urban children. Village life, after all, is the most companionable yet devised. Humanity's immemorial gossip seems a small price to pay in exchange for humanity itself. Unlike the inhabitants of a large town, all villagers recognise one another by sight, by name, by reputation. If they have deserved it, they will be remembered lovingly by their neighbours' grandchildren. In short, they belong; they know and are known.

Castle Acre's showpiece lies at the end of a metalled cul-de-sac which passes the site of a Roman camp, a medieval church, and the husk of a hilltop castle. Then, in a combe beside the River Mar, the west front of a ruined priory rises from close-cropped lawns. The effect seems doubly dramatic because the front itself is merely a thin façade of red sandstone, a silhouette without depth. Nothing lies beyond it, except a tracery of broken pillars and shattered walls, pinned back like paper on the sky. The best preserved portion—the prior's house—was enlarged three centuries ago, and eventually became the home of a family of farmhands. In 1970 a member of that family, the last occupant of the prior's house, was living in the village. Dissolved in 1537, the priory passed to the Duke of Northumberland and thence to Sir Edward Coke, ancestor of the Earl of Leicester who in 1929 granted supervision of the priory to the Ministry of Works.

Castle Acre Priory was founded by the Earl and Countess of Surrey, who, while making a pilgrimage to Rome, were caught between the rival armies of France and the Papacy. Seeking shelter at the Abbey of Cluny, the earl was so impressed by the monks' piety that he obtained their abbot's permission to found the first Cluniac house in England, the Priory of St Pancras, near his castle at Lewes in Sussex. Soon afterwards he founded Castle Acre Priory as a daughter house. The average modern man dismisses monasticism as Milton dismissed it, 'a fugitive and cloistered virtue'. He either does not know or has ceased to care that for nearly a thousand years the majority of monks were devout and hardworking craftsmen, farmers, teachers, scholars, artists. Each of the several Orders specialised in a form of good works. The Cistercians became the finest sheep breeders in Christendom, while the Cluniacs won renown for the splendour of their church services, the *Opus Dei* or 'Work of God'. Despite the varying customs and traditions, almost every monastery owed something to an Italian nobleman, St Benedict, who imposed on his own Order the threefold vows of poverty, celibacy, obedience, together with at least seven hours' manual labour each day. His motto, in fact, was *Laborare est orare* ('Work is prayer'). Every religious house offered food, shelter, and medical care to guests; charging them according to their means (no means, no charge). It was the monks who kept the lamp of culture burning during the Dark Ages of civil war and barbarian invasion. Long before printing was invented, they wrote histories and biographies, as well as copying and illuminating texts of many Latin and Greek writers, for lack of which the world would be immeasurably poorer. Monks, indeed, were among the relatively few medieval Englishmen who could read and write. Like Bede, they were historians; like Caedmon, they were poets; like Occam, philosophers; like Bacon, scientists. They alone provided such education as was available; offering it not only to the poor, from whom they drew their own successors, but also to Kings and noblemen. Alfred the Great was educated by the monks of Sherborne; at Ely, as we have seen, the monks educated King Edward the Confessor.

During the later Middle Ages, however, monasticism lapsed from arduous piety into idle worldliness. The whole Church became tainted, not least because many of its bishops acted as senior civil servants in a government that was turning away from the medieval ideal of a united Christendom, and becoming nationally selfconscious. Even if the Reformation had never occurred, the number of religious houses would have dwindled, and their cultural role would have passed to the universities. Nevertheless, our debt to the best of the medieval monks is incalculable. England on the eve of the Reformation contained more than two thousand religious houses. Today not one of them remains intact, and most have disappeared.

The Peddars Way, by contrast, has not disappeared. On the contrary, I saw it shining like a metalled sunbeam leading north-north-west from the Earl of Surrey's gatehouse. For three miles I followed it, marvelling at the precision of its course. The Romans, however, did not favour straightness at any price. Faced by an extensive swamp, they would generally bypass it rather than accept the task of drainage. If a Celtic track went their way, they might co-opt it into the new road, straightening and widening en route. Narrow rivers were spanned by means of a bridge slung across moored boats; wide rivers, by a bridge on stakes. When the Romans left Britain, the natives and the immigrants allowed the paved roads to become green roads. So slow were the English to learn, that in 300 AD a wagonload of goods travelled from London to York more quickly than a similar load in 1700AD.

About three miles beyond Castle Acre the Ordnance map marks a place called Shepherds Bush. Shepherds may indeed have gathered there long ago, but not even their ghosts have ever appeared on any of my own journeys to the spot. From Shepherds Bush the lane veered toward Great Massingham (a picture postcard village with several ponds and thatched cottages) while Peddars Way kept straight on, this time as a green road through fields famous for their fertility. 'This part of England,' wrote Defoe, 'is also remarkable for being the first where the feeding and fattening of cattle, both sheep as well as black cattle, with turnips, was first practis'd in England ...'. Norfolk was certainly the home of two eminent agriculturalists, Thomas Tusser and Thomas Coke. The former cultivated Abbey Farm at West Dereham, where he composed several Tudor textbooks in verse, including *Five Hundneth pointes of good husbandry*, which he advertised in his own epitaph:

Here Thomas Tusser, clad in earth, doth lie,
Who sometimes made the Points of Husbandry ...

The second farmer, Thomas Coke, was a descendant of Sir Edward Coke, the jurist, who in 1510 built the manor house at Holkham, only a short distance from the sea. In the years when I was a farm pupil, we regarded Coke as a radical innovator. Recent scholarship, on the other hand, suggests that he owed much of his success to an adroit use of traditional methods. In 1734 he built the present Holkham Hall, on ground that was described by Thomas Crabbe, the Suffolk parson-poet:

There poppies, nodding, mock the hope of toil;
There the blue bugloss paints the sterile soil.

They say that Coke's farming career began when one of his tenants refused to renew a lease at five shillings per acre, protesting that the soil was too sour; whereupon Coke farmed the land himself, patiently transforming the district into England's richest corn and cattle country. His contemporary, Nathaniel Kent, complimented him, saying that the income from the Holkham estate had been improved 'in the memory of man, from five to up upwards of twenty thousand pounds a year ... and is still increasing like a snow ball. Mr. Coke, the present owner of it, is a real friend to agriculture ...'. Being a crony of the King, Coke could have acquired a title simply by asking, but he held a low opinion of many of the people who did acquire a title. The King seems to have shared that view, because, whenever he wished to dissuade Coke from a course of action, he would say: 'Coke, if you do that thing, I shall knight you'. In the end, as a sop to his family, Coke submitted to become Earl of Leicester. Not the least remarkable thing about him was his hale longevity. At the age of seventy or thereabouts he married Lady Anne Keppel, by whom he had four sons and a daughter. He died in 1842, at the age of ninety.

But again we have wandered, and must rejoin the Peddars Way. Northward it went, sometimes clearly defined as a green road; at other times narrow and obscure, occasionally obliterated by ploughing, yet always sequestered. Only once in five visitations have I met a fellow-traveller on the Peddars Way, and he was a farmhand. Like Romney Marsh, this part of Norfolk was frequented by smugglers who used the Way as an escape into a territory that was as unoccupied then as it is now.

The Way's original pavement had long since sunk from sight, buried beneath centuries of tillage. Only the course was visible, an emblem of Rome's legacy of roads, villas, dykes, duty, discipline, fortitude, law. Jurisprudence, indeed, was the Romans' greatest intellectual achievement, being to them as philosophy was to the Greeks, and as religion to the Jews. Rome created and codified law with a skill unsurpassed in the history of mankind. Although the medieval English jurists discarded most of the Roman forms, preferring to create new laws by means of royal writs, they were undoubtedly inspired by the spirit of Roman jurisprudence as expressed in Justinian's *Digest*: 'Law is the art of the good and the just'. Our Admiralty Courts retained certain features of Roman law until the fourteenth century. Scottish law still does retain some of those features, and the concept of *res publica* or 'commonweal' is still acknowledged by English courts.

It would have been pleasant to linger by the Way, but the sun now said 'After noon', and the dog and I had several miles to go. From the summit of the next hill I boxed the Norfolk compass, with the mind's eye seeing those places which had contributed a footnote to English history. I saw Sheringham, a redbrick Victorian seaside resort, still a quiet and dignified place. I saw Holt, another and older town, whose school was endowed in 1555 by Sir Thomas Gresham, Lord Mayor of London, and whose pupils included Benjamin Britten and W. H. Auden. Blakeney I saw, that landfall for yachtsmen and ornithologists, with two-towered church, ancient guildhall, and a narrow street delving to a bristle of waterside masts. Blickling, too, appeared, deep in wooded country, where Lord Chief Justice Hobart built a mansion, the childhood home of Anne Boleyn. Those and many others came to mind, each with its own memory of summer and of winter, of gay times and of sad, of war and of peace. Which among them should I revisit?

While I was trying to answer that question, the Peddars Way passed within sight of Anmer, the *aened mere* or 'duck pond' on the edge of a royal estate. Sandringham, which was bought in 1861 by the Prince of Wales, who demolished the modest house, and raised a mansion on the site. Like Balmoral Castle, Sandringham House is a private residence, not an official palace. King George V loved Sandringham even more than his father had loved it: 'Dear old Sandringham,' he wrote, 'the place I love better than anywhere else in the world'. At Sandringham he spent his honeymoon; there his second son was born; and there, as he would have wished, he died ('The King's life is drawing peacefully to its close'). The next King, Edward VIII—a lover of gay and sometimes gaudy people—disliked Sandringham, and might have sold it had he reigned long enough. George VI, on the other hand, inherited his father's love of the estate. He, too, died there, in his sleep, after a long illness bravely borne. Her present Majesty, Queen Elizabeth II, graciously opens the grounds of Sandringham, so that her subjects may share the gardens where the Sovereign can briefly forget those cares of State which Henry VIII called 'London business'.

Invigorated by the perfect Maytime weather, I felt able to walk forever, or at any rate until Hesperus called it a day. But again I remembered that we must cover several more miles before we could dismount from Shanks's pony. Soon the Peddars began to flow downhill, like a green river to the sea. Ahead of us, on the skyline above Fring, stood a ruined windmill, the ghost of a vanished order. Domesday Book makes no mention of windmills; it seems that in 1086 all the mills were watermills. The first reliable reference to a windmill occurred in 1185, when a mill at Weedley in Yorkshire was leased at eight shillings yearly. In 1919 more than three hundred such mills were working; in 1946, less than fifty. Thereafter a number of individuals set about the task of salvaging the wreckage. As a result, Norfolk and Suffolk in 1977 contained some twenty windmills that were either working or well preserved. Fring's ruined windmill seemed to rise higher while the Roman road went down, down, down, away from green solitude, onto a metalled lane and thence north-west to Little Walsingham, the *ham* or 'settlement' whose chief was *Waels*. At Walsingham an Englishman discovers one of his remote ancestors, because the son of *Waels* (a Viking hero, Sigemund) is mentioned in *Beowulf*, the Anglo-Saxon verse saga.

Little Walsingham is a village of timber and tile and brick, handsome in its own right. Throughout the Middle Ages it ranked next after Canterbury as place of English pilgrimage. Tradition says that in 1061 the lady of the manor, Richeldis de

Faverches, saw a vision of the Virgin Mary, who commanded her to build a replica of the House of the Annunciation at Nazareth, where Jesus is supposed to have lived as a child. Richeldis obeyed, and the replica was placed in a chapel. Her son, Geoffrey, endowed the shrine with lands which passed to his chaplain, Edwy, who founded a priory nearby. In 1512 Erasmus described the shrine as 'a little chapel sealed over with wood; on either side a little door where the pilgrims go through . . . meet for saints, all things be so bright with gold, silver, and precious stones'. Medieval Walsingham was a blend of faith, piety, and fraud. Thus, when John Paston fell ill in 1443 his wife wrote to assure him that 'My mother behested another image of wax of the weight of you to our lady of Walsingham . . .'. At about the same time a certain Margery Hackster, wife of a Norfolk carpenter, declared that no Christian ought to make any kind of pilgrimage, 'neither to our Lady of Walsingham nor to any other saint or place'. When Henry VIII ordered the shrine to be desecrated, eleven local people were executed because they had protested. In 1921 a replica of the shrine was erected in the parish church, followed ten years later by a chapel. The shrine is now visited annually by thousands of people from many parts of the world.

Beyond Little Walsingham the lane skirted the park of Holkham Hall, where Thomas Coke gave new life to English agriculture. After about six miles of deep seclusion I reached the birthplace of Vice-Admiral Viscount Nelson, Duke of Bronte, sixth of twelve children of the rector of Burnham Thorpe, a village which at first sight appears to be inhabited only by the landlord of the Nelson Arms and the occupier of the adjacent Trafalgar Stores. Across the fields, however, you catch sight of the parish church, whose rector in 1377 was Edmund de Walpole, an ancestor of England's first prime minister. Inside the church are a letter written by Nelson, dated 'Victory, May 14th 1804', and a rood screen made of oak from the *Victory*, presented by the people of Canada. On feast days the church tower unfurls a replica of Nelson's flag at the Battle of the Nile.

The house in which Nelson was born stood on the edge of the village, facing a stream that was dammed in order to create a pool on which young Nelson sailed his model ships. Beside the stream is a signpost: *Site of Nelson's Birthplace*. On my first arrival, in 1967, the signpost was so dingy that I removed some of the moss. Nelson's old home was a sizeable L-shaped building with large garden and a croquet lawn. In 1802 it was demolished by a rich incumbent who designed a new house nearby. In 1956 yet another rectory was built, closer to the church. In 1928, when some plants from Nelson's garden were presented to the United States Naval Academy in Maryland, the Admiral Superintendent acknowledged the gift by making a signal: 'The American Navy in its inception was largely modelled after the Royal Navy and we have found in our generous rivals the most helpful friends. It is eminently fitting that these plants from the great Nelson's garden should take root and be cherished in the United States Naval Academy as a symbol of our close relationship with the illustrious Admiral'.

When Nelson was only twelve years old he enlisted as midshipman in *HMS Raisonnable* commanded by his uncle, Captain Maurice Suckling RN, who had tried to dissuade the child's father: 'What,' he asked, 'has poor Horace done, who is so weak, that he above all the rest should be sent to rough it out at sea?'. Absence, however, did not dim fondness. Writing from the *Victory*, only a few months before his death, Nelson confessed: 'Most probably I shall never see dear, dear Burnham again . . .'. Nelson's supreme achievement was to save England from invasion by Bonaparte, the dictator of Europe. This he did by defeating the French fleet off Cape Trafalgar. While his own ships were preparing to engage the enemy, Nelson scribbled a prayer in his pocket book:

> May the great God, whom I worship, grant to my Country, and for the benefit of Europe in general, a great and glorious Victory; and may no misconduct in anyone tarnish it; and may humanity after Victory be the predominent feature in the British Fleet.

On the quarterdeck, when action was imminent, Nelson made the most famous signal in our history: 'England expects that every man will do his duty'. An hour later, having defeated the enemy, Nelson died of wounds. His last words were: 'Thank God, I have done my duty'.

At Burnham Thorpe I was only a few miles from the Wash, which separates East Anglia from the North Country. It would therefore have been easy to reach the next lap of my journey by turning north-west into Lincolnshire and Yorkshire; but once again I made a pilgrimage, this time doubling back to Holme-next-the-Sea and thence eastward for a mile or so to Brancaster, the site of *Branodunum*, a Roman camp between the sea and the coastal road. Garrisoned by Dalmatian cavalry, *Branodunum* served as a fort of the Saxon Shore, ready to repel Teutonic pirates. The concept of a Saxon Shore was formed by Carausius, Admiral of the Romano-British fleet, who eventually took part in the piracy he was supposed to suppress. The tactics and strategy of the Saxon Shore were amphibious because the Romans never excelled as sailors. English seamanship is a legacy from Celts, Vikings, and Teutons. The task of the Roman galleys was to reconnoitre rather than to repel. If invaders did land, they were engaged by troops from the nearest fort. Of *Branodunum* only a green mound remains. All else has disappeared ... the watch towers, the granary, the baths, the men's quarters, the commander's house. Yet the Roman legacy survives in every Christian church, for it was a Roman Emperor, Constantine, who raised Christianity from the miseries of a persecuted sect to the role of Europe's official religion. In Norfolk the clerical legacy is especially rich because the county was for centuries a granary, market garden, wool staple, and cloth factory. East Anglian merchants spent part of their wealth on building splendid churches, chiefly of flint, the only material readily available to most of the region. In 1977 the Norfolk Society's Committee for Country Churches was rescuing some of those masterpieces from redundancy and decay.

What of East Anglia's future? Even fifty years ago a traveller through England might with reasonable assurance have predicted the state of an area as it would be fifty years after his own death. Today no such assurance is possible. Places which seemed safe have succumbed. In Yorkshire, for example, thousands of acres near Selby are being developed as a coalfield. Some of the loveliest parts of Dorset are being developed as an oilfield. Every year, too, thousands of acres of moorland are being either cultivated or urbanised. Large tracts of the Home

Counties, which in 1940 were ploughland and pasture, have disappeared under bricks and mortar. No spot is safe. Even the so-called areas of outstanding natural beauty have been pockmarked by industry and tourism. East Anglia is among those victims. Humberside now spills a spate of lorries and factories from the north. Thetford—lately a small country town—is ringed by so many industrial sites that traffic lights now control the carborne workers, many of whom never saw East Anglia until a job led them there. Norwich itself is menaced; and in Suffolk the once-rural city of Ipswich has been taken over by a regime whose 'business executives' pay £10,000 for a cottage that was built for £50. Such things are inevitable when a standard of living means always a standard of spending, never a standard of 'plain living and high thinking'. Meanwhile, international Marxism nods approvingly at the Western

Harbridge, Hampshire

'Off the beaten track' is an old and useful phrase. It was probably coined as a literal statement by travellers who had pioneered their own path. Today the phrase serves as a synonym for any sequestered and little known place, like this off-beat hamlet. The word 'hamlet' comes from the Middle English *hamelet*, meaning 'small village'. It is almost a definition of a hamlet to say that it has neither a shop nor a church nor an inn, and that the population seldom exceeds one hundred. Sir Walter Scott described a hamlet as a settlement where 'thirty or forty families dwelt together'.

When we say that people in a hamlet must seek 'life' at their nearest town, we assume that 'life' is a question of numbers. This is a fallacy. Every countryman knows that companionship may be stronger in a hamlet than in a city, for whereas most people in a city are strangers to one another, all people in a hamlet know and are known.

bourgeois intellectuals who kow-tow to any tyranny—or, rather, to any Socialist tyranny—that offers its captive masses a larger plate of subsidised food and a smaller dose of personal enterprise. Après nous le deluge? Perhaps; yet hope springs to the breast of eternal compassion, and an Englishman must trust that his fellow countrymen will recover their senses while they still possess some to recover.

My East Anglian journey ended at Holme-next-the-Sea, a village of brick-and-flint cottages, church, shop, inn, and Roman road, the Peddars Way, terminating as a track among sand dunes on a deserted shore. There, or somewhere close by, the Way was once served by a Roman ferry that carried travellers over the Wash to Lincolnshire and thence to York and the wild country beyond Hadrian's Wall.

Potter Higham, Norfolk

'Railways, the wonder of our Age, have begun a journey of infinite length. It is impossible to imagine that they can ever be outpaced by some new mode of travel.' So wrote a Victorian journalist. And *we* have lived to see the impossible come true.

The decline began when nationalisation abolished the multi-coloured regional liveries and robbed the railway worker of pride in his own line. Today our railways have priced themselves beyond the purse of many who prefer to travel by car. High speed trains do not counterbalance the slovenly stations, the drab rolling stock, the delayed departures and late arrivals that are inflicted on millions of commuters.

This derelict station was part of the Great Eastern Railway, opened in 1863. The dark blue engines had scarlet coupling rods, white cab roof, and polished brass and copperwork. Electric trains are faster and cleaner than steam, yet those old locomotives wove a potent spell. As Siegfried Sassoon said:

with them goes
The clamour of their journeying; while those
Who sped them stand to wave a last farewell.

89

5 THE NORTH EAST

In Lincolnshire you overhear the voice of Tennyson's Northern Farmer:

> Dubbut loak at the waste, theer warn't not fead for a cow;
> Nowt at all but bracken an' furze, an' looak at it now . . .
> Fourscore yows upon it, an' some on it doon to sead.

Only northerners say 'nowt' and 'dubbut'. Out of its own mouth, therefore, Lincolnshire asserts a northern lineage.

Like Yorkshire, the county is so large that it was long ago divided into three administrative regions—Lindsey, Kestevern, Holland—of which the last contains nearly 27,000 acres of Fens. Driving from Norfolk to Sleaford, you feel that those fens are infinite because inescapable. At Sleaford, however, you find that the Lincolnshire churches are as a rule larger than those in Norfolk. Among the Sleaford memorials is a brass to George Carre, a Tudor merchant. The next generation of Carres acquired a knighthood, and one of them became Chancellor of the duchy of Lancaster. Another family of Lincolnshire merchants, the de la Poles, achieved a duke's coronet and a cardinal's hat. Thus did the flexible English class system avoid the revolution which destroyed the inflexible French caste system.

Somewhere beyond Sleaford you notice a change of scene, comparable with the change beyond Littleport. Trees become more plentiful, and the lanes climb as though to prove that Lincolnshire is not wholly a fen. It was from one of those steep lanes that I sighted Lincoln, the Roman *Lindon Colonia*, now a conglomeration of factories, offices, warehouses, and railway yards. Above that dismal prospect stands the cathedral, perched on a rocky eminence overlooking the city. In one mood you might liken it to an aristocrat gazing *de haut en bas*, conscious that his lineage had existed before the factories appeared, and would remain after the factories had disappeared. In another mood you might liken it to a supplicant, pleading to England as Jesus pleaded to Israel: 'O Jerusalem, Jerusalem, thou that killest the prophets, and stonest them which are sent unto thee, how often would I have gathered thy children together, even as a hen gathereth her chickens under her wings, and ye would not!' And in a third mood you might liken it to Shakespeare's Lear, 'a foolish, fond old man', who supposes himself to be still a powerful King, though in truth he is already an ancient monument.

Consecrated in 1092, Lincoln Cathedral suffered an earth tremor which caused the surveyor to condemn the fabric with two words: *Scissa est.* Twelve months later the rebuilding was begun by a new bishop, St Hugh of Avalon, formerly Treasurer of *La Grande Chartreuse*. In its heyday the diocese stretched as far south as Oxfordshire. Seen as I was seeing it, Lincoln Cathedral symbolised the deepest difference between England before the Industrial Revolution and England after it. Throughout the Middle Ages and until the early years of the twentieth century, most Englishfolk believed that the Universe was created purposefully by a benign God, and that their earthly suffering, if it were faithfully borne, would be eclipsed by their heavenly bliss. Sinners they were indeed, yet penitents also, and therefore worthy to join 'the communion of saints'. Among many Englishfolk nowadays those beliefs have been supplanted either by thoughtlessness or by Bertrand Russell's *credo*: 'That man is the product of causes which had no prevision of the end they were achieving; that his origin and growth, his hopes and fears, his loves and beliefs are but the outcome of accidental collactions of atoms; that all the labour of the ages, all the devotion, all the inspiration, all the noon-day brightness of human genius, are destined to extinction in the vast death of the solar system'. Unlike Bertrand Russell, I was never admitted into the ultimate secrets of existence, and must therefore be content to state a commonplace, as follows: Time will show whether the new bleak creed can act like a catalyst, arousing a sense of brotherhood among men who are equally doomed, or whether it will persuade

91

an even greater number of them to eat, drink, and be as merry as is possible among occupants of the condemned cell.

Lincoln first became important in AD 47, when it served as a fort from which the Romans deterred the East Anglian Iceni and the northern Brigantes. About twenty years later the fort became a *colonia* or settlement of retired soldiers, covering forty acres on the hill. One imperial relic, the Newport Arch, is the oldest city gateway in use in Britain. From Lincoln the Romans built two roads, Ermine Street (leading north to York) and Foss Way (leading south to Devon). In 1954 I rode a horse along the entire length of the Foss, passing through Newark, Leicester, and Bath. Had I tried to repeat the ride in 1977 I would probably have been run over within sight of Lincoln Cathedral.

Meanwhile, the fenny country accompanied me as far as Epworth, birthplace of John Wesley, the fifteenth of nineteen children of the rector, Samuel Wesley, whose home was burned by a Radical mob. Undeterred, the rector rebuilt the present mansion (now a Wesleyan museum), which has fifty windows, and bears the Arms that the Wesleys acquired during the Crusades. At the age of twenty-four, John Wesley became a Fellow of Lincoln College, Oxford, and might have enjoyed a brilliant academic career, but preferred to serve as his father's curate at Wroot, a hamlet of Epworth. In those years the winter floods sometimes forced the rector to travel by boat. Writing to John, he complained: 'I am *hipp'd* by my voyage and journey to and from Epworth last Sunday; being lamed by having my breeches too full of water, partly from a downfall from a thunder shower, and partly from the wash over the boat . . .'

Epworth has not greatly changed since John Wesley lived there. He would recognise the straggling street, the base of a market cross, the Red Lion, the avenue leading to his father's church. The population remains constant at about two thousand. Wesley himself is widely regarded as a Radical dissenter, despite the fact that he lived and died as a High Tory and an Anglican priest. His mission was not to found a new sect but to arouse an old Church, at a time when many of the clergy were insensitive to the welfare of those whose need was greatest. By reviling Wesley, the Church made it easy for him to attract a large following of artisans, farmhands, and shopkeepers, whose dislike of the Church was political rather than doctrinal, since few of them could define the theological opinions of Zwingli and Calvin and Melancthon. Although they were bigoted, the best of such noncomformists possessed an innate dignity, and by their common sense they were able to control those who would have plunged the kingdom into violent rebellion. As leaders of the first trades unions they advocated moderate reform; as Liberals they combined personal integrity with civic restraint. Yet the paradox remains, that a Tory priest should have fostered a creed which in our day has become Socialist secularism.

John Wesley stands supreme among travellers in Britain. At a time when eight miles an hour was a fair speed, he covered more than a quarter of a million miles, chiefly on horseback, visiting almost every part of these islands. He made forty-two journeys to Ireland, and twenty-five to Scotland. In America he travelled and preached widely. At the age of seventy he was delivering fifteen sermons a week, and riding thirty miles a day. 'I must,' he declared, 'be on horseback for life if I am to be healthy.' He *was* on horseback for life, or at any rate until he reached his eighties, when he travelled by coach. Wesley's *Journal* is unique among British travelogues. A preface explains why he wrote it: 'It was in pursuance of an advice by Bishop Taylor, in his "Rules for Holy Living and Dying" that, about fifteen years ago, I began to take a more exact account than I had done before, of the manner wherein I spent my time, writing down how I had employed every hour'. Yet the thousands of printed pages in the *Journal* are only 'a short extract of those particulars which I wrote for my own use only, and which would answer no valuable end to others, however important they were to me'. In his eighty-eighth year he was still preaching, though by now so frail that, in the words of an eye witness, 'on each side of him stood two friends, and the two held him up ... His feeble voice was barely audible, but his reverend countenance formed a picture never to be forgotten'. John Wesley was the most influential Englishman in the history of religion.

The lane from Epworth to Wroot is devious and quiet. In 1962 and again in 1975 I found the hamlet silent and apparently unpeopled. Perhaps they were all at work in the fields, farming hereabouts being the chief occupation. Wesley's medieval church at Wroot was superseded in 1876 by a small and ugly redbrick building.

Wroot is Lincolnshire's most westerly parish, forming part of the Isle of Axholme, the *holm* or 'dry land' among fens near the village of Haxey. The word 'holm' comes from the Old Norse *holmr*, the Old Swedish *holmber*, and the Old Danish *holm*. In short, I had reached Viking country, that sinewy strand in England's pedigree. By sailing up the Humber and the Wash the Vikings were able to conquer a large area of northern England and to impose a tax, *Danegeld*, promising in return not to extend their conquests. When the Vikings demanded more money, the natives meekly paid it, whereafter, according to the law of industrial relations, the screw was turned even tighter. Most of the Vikings who settled in England were Danes; the rest were either Swedes or Norwegians. The meaning of their collective name is uncertain. Some philologists trace it to *vik*, the 'creek' from which the invaders sailed; others trace it to *vig*, the 'battle' which they fought on landing; others, again, trace it to *wic*, the 'camp' which they built as a base for their incursions.

From the edge of Wroot's unpeopled solitude I took one pace forward into Yorkshire, another Viking name, based on the Saxon *Eoforwic* or 'place of boars', which was pronounced by the Vikings as *Iorvik* and ultimately as York. Yorkshiremen will tell you that there are as many acres in their county as there are words in the Bible. The county itself is certainly our largest, straddling England from the North Sea to a point near the Irish Sea. From its northernmost summits you can sight the Scottish hills; from its southernmost summits you can sight the Midland smoke. The population is twice that of Wales, and a million more than Denmark's; in all, about five million. Because of its size, the county was trisected into three administrative Ridings, a corruption of the Saxon *thing* or 'judicial asembly'. The largest Riding, the West, was seventy thousand acres larger than Lincolnshire; the smallest Riding, the East, was twice the size of Bedfordshire. In 1974 the trio of proud and ancient Ridings was destroyed by Act of Parliament.

To enter Yorkshire is not necessarily to shake off the Fens. My own entry brought me to Hatfield, a village of mellow brick houses in a region so swampy that Vermuyden was commissioned to drain it. Thereafter I joined a race track, formerly called the Great North Road, one of a famous company . . . Dover Road, Portsmouth Road, Brighton Road, Bath Road, Holyhead Road. Old men can remember when each of those highways was unmistakably itself. Their fathers knew the roads when each maintained its own colourful stage coaches, its painted inn signs, its farmfolk who seldom ventured beyond the nearest market town. Today those roads are for the most part identical race tracks whereon the scurrying ant may easily forget whether he has just left Luton or is about to enter Bridgwater.

By keeping to the eastern side of Yorkshire I avoided Barnsley, Bradford, Brighouse, Halifax, Huddersfield, Dewsbury, and Leeds, where one century of mechanisation wrought more change than England had witnessed since the Norman Conquest. Unlike our own technological revolution, which seeps into every household, the industrial revolution was at first so localised that a shepherd within six miles of Keighley lived much as his Tudor forebears had lived, though Keighley itself was already an industrial hive. Mechanical inventions multiplied as never before. Within a single lifetime the population of England rose from six to thirteen million while hordes of craftsmen and farmhands trekked to the factories and mean streets of industrial towns. In 1825 a northern newspaper made this happy announcement: 'To the Overseers of the Poor and families desirous of settling in Macclesfield. Wanted between 4,000 and 5,000 persons between the ages of 7 and 21'. In 1842 a Royal Commission reported on the northern coalfields: 'In many pits children were employed at six years old; in some at five, and in one case a child of three was found to be employed'. Inspired by Lord Shaftesbury, several eminent Tories tried to shame the national conscience. Carlyle declared: 'British industrial existence seems fast becoming one huge poison-swamp of reeking pestilence, both physical and spiritual'. Kingsley declared: 'The Church, the gentlemen, and the workmen should be ranged against the Manchester School'. Disraeli, indicting the mercantile Whigs, declared: 'their duties to the social system seem altogether omitted'. By those were voices crying in a wilderness of industrial euphoria. For the first time in history the merchants and the manufacturers became the masters of

England, the men who sacrificed agriculture on the altar of industry. A farmer who had been born when England was still exporting wheat, died when she was already importing it.

Somewhere along the concrete race track I met the full force of a hurricane which in 1912 Edward Thomas had detected as a slight breeze: 'Motor cars,' he wrote, 'tyrannically owned the road'. It is indeed a daunting and a deafening experience to stand beside a busy highway while the traffic thunders past, oblivious alike of the landscape and of any traveller in distress. How clearly Edward Thomas foresaw the menace of the motorway: 'Such a road,' he warned, 'is tiring, because either the eye or the mind's eye sees long or taunting or menacing lengths before it, and is brought into conflict with its sheer distance, and the mind is continually trying to carry the body over this distance . . . and being again and again defeated, and more and more conscious of defeat, becomes irritated, if not numbed, by the importunate monotony.' Once again, therefore, I relieved the *longueurs* by recalling some earlier journeys through more restful parts of Yorkshire. I remembered the bluff coast at Whitby, and the moors that surged like a heathery sea on either side of the road to Pickering. What comely villages cluster in those dales. During my childhood they were unvisited throughout the year, except by a few walkers and cyclists. Even today they dwell at peace between October and April. I remembered the village of Rosedale Abbey, watered by the River Seven, flanked by near-mountainous moorland. Some of the cottages beside the green were built of stone from a ruined abbey which Robert de Stuteville founded in the twelfth century. The Vikings called the place *hrossa-delr* or 'vale of horses'. I remembered also Holderness, that lonely coastal zone northward from Hull and eastward from Beverley. There the sea had swept away whole towns, and is still stealing several feet of cliff each year. Its most notable victim was Ravenspur, a town with five churches, two gates, and a leper house founded by the Knights Hospitallers. Ravenspur today lies under the sea, deep as Debussy's *Cathedrale Engloute*.

But those pleasant memories could not outlast the present wretched rat-race. I began to feel as weary as Celia Fiennes when she wrote: 'here I was most sensible of the long Yorkshire

miles ... much longer miles than other parts'. Her weariness
was justified because—although the English mile had been
defined in 1595 as 1,760 yards—large areas of the north country
retained the old British mile, which was nearly one-and-a-half
miles. Weariness, however, gave way to wariness when a squall
smothered the windscreen, but without slackening the maniacs'
speed. Then the clouds passed, and were pursued by an arc of
blue sky which transformed every twig into a chandelier, each
raindrop reflecting a spectrum. When at last I reached York, the
city was bathed in light and shade, part blue and smiling, part
grey and scowling.

York was *Eboracum*, Britain's premier city and a Roman
spearhead against the Brigantes, the most powerful of all the
northern tribes. Four Emperors visited York; one of them,
Constantine, was formally proclaimed there. *Eboracum* has
vanished, except for some fragments of its wall, and the lower
part of a tower. The rest lies buried beneath the medieval city
and later development. To wander through York is to enter the
Middle Ages and their Tudor aftermath: Fishergate, Walmgate,
Micklegate, Monkgate; the Hall of the Merchant Adventurers,
timbered and timeproof; the King's Manor, calm as a cloister;
Clifford's Tower, alone on a knoll; a warren of narrow streets
from whose upper windows the citizens could almost shake
hands across the cobbles; and the minster itself, the north
country's supreme achievement in stone. A handful of York's
forty-one medieval churches survive and are memorable in their
own right, but they are dwarfed by Britain's largest cathedral,
the work of two-and-a-half centuries (from 1220 until 1472),
covering 25,000 square feet. In 1829 the minster was severely
damaged by lunatic arson. During the 1960s it was found to be
topheavy because the medieval masons had built on ground that
was less than reliable. When, therefore, a later generation added
the massive central tower, both the fabric and the foundation
faltered under excessive stress. A worldwide appeal was
launched, soliciting millions of pounds wherewith to undertake a
rescue operation that would occupy several years. In 1969 the
Dean of York conducted me on a tour of the restoration.
Standing below the level of the floor, I looked up at the soaring
pillars and then down at their splintered bases.

The Archbishop of York is sometimes described as 'The Primate'. But that is misleading because England has two Primates, the Archbishop of York (Primate of England) and the Archbishop of Canterbury (Primate of All England). That distinction was devised during the Middle Ages by Archbishop Islip of Canterbury and Archbishop Thoresby of York, the latter yielding precedence without foregoing dignity. The medieval archbishops were Princes of the Church, wielding immense power, both temporal and spiritual. The most famous Archbishop of York, Cardinal Wolsey, was the richest man in England. Today the two archbishops receive a stipend which an airpilot would regard as petty cash. Each is styled 'His Grace', and each sits in the House of Lords. The Archbishop of Canterbury takes precedence before all the nobility and all the great officers of State; the Archbishop of York ranks next after the Lord Chancellor. In 1970 the Archbishop of York was Dr Coggan, with whom I had been at school. He received me very kindly in his palace on the outskirts of York, where we spent some time discussing 'Pongo' (our old headmaster), and 'DBD' (the Rugger international who coached us to invincibility), and Lord Clive (who gave his name to one of our School Houses), and the Hebrew Class (which for more than three hundred years had elevated several of our schoolfellows to the bench of bishops). We even recalled the bearded French chef who supplied The Lun or tuckshop with succulent eclairs.

North of York I joined Dere Street, the Roman road from *Eboracum* to *Trimontium* or Newstead in Scotland. Parts of the road were scarcely wider than a lane through deep country; other parts had been overlaid by a dual carriageway, as at Scotch Corner, a screeching roundabout. Thereafter the road resumed its quiet course, leaving the commercial travellers to pursue their race. What a relief it is—both a tonic and a sedative—to escape from a main road. I celebrated my own escape by leaning on a gate, listening to the myriad sounds which compose a rural stillness. How many blackbirds, I wondered, were at that moment singing to silent bluebells? All over England they sang, and all over England the bluebells shone. It so happened that I had chosen to rest within sight of a bridge over the River Tees (Celtic *teas* or 'surging'). Across the water lay another border, this time into County Durham and the village of Piercebridge (from the Middle English *persh*, meaning 'osiers'). Unlike the crossing from Kent into Sussex, the border between Yorkshire and Durham reveals an instant change of scene and sound. The former is visible at Piercebridge itself, a small and neat village with several red sandstone cottages beside a green. Here the accent changes from north Yorkshire to south Durham, a variation difficult to describe. For example, whereas Yorkshire pronounces 'stone' as something like 'storn', in Durham the sound resembles 'stane'. Whence came this variety of accent? A half-answer is supplied by philologists, who recognise five major dialects that were spoken in England a thousand years ago; namely, South Eastern, Southern, West Midland, East Midland, Northern. Each dialect was in many ways a different language, so that a twelfth-century Durham seaman would have sounded almost unintelligible to a Dorset shepherd, and utterly meaningless to a Cornish miner. Yet none of this explains why the words and music still vary from county to county and also within a county. Thus, in 1976 a farrier at Kirkby Lonsdale assured me that he could identify the men of Kendal simply by listening to them. Yet Kendal and Kirkby are both in the ancient county of Westmorland, and less than a dozen miles apart. I doubt that anyone ever will account for those facts. Their origins are too remote, and may have been too particular.

The origins of County Durham, by contrast, can be traced to the ninth century AD, when the King of Northumbria granted a large area of land to the Congregation of St Cuthbert. Two centuries later, William the Conqueror made the region into a County Palatine or *palatinium*, the name of a senior judicial officer of the Merovingian Kings. To ensure that none of his subjects should become over-powerful, William limited the amount of land which any one person might hold in any one district. Throughout the far north, however, and along the Welsh Marches, the presence of hostile tribes forced him to create vice-regencies which he entrusted either to his kinsmen or to the most faithful of his other friends. Thus it was that County Durham came to be governed by the Prince-Bishops of Durham, who acted as viceroys, commanding their own army, coining their own money, administering their own law. Not until 1873 was the jurisdiction of Durham's Court of Pleas transferred to London. Several palatinate privileges have survived, as in the Court of Chancery of the County Palatine of Durham, which continues to act on behalf of the Crown. The last of the Prince-Bishops, William van Mildert, died in 1836, having founded Durham University, whose academic gowns are called Palatine Purple.

Durham reveals a blend of populous industry and sequestered farmland. Nearly half the county is a coalfield; large parts of the rest are moorland. Often I have walked for hours on those moors, seeing neither a house nor a human being. Several times each year I used to drive from Kirkby Lonsdale to Middleton-in-Teesdale, and on each journey the lane seemed to grow wilder and lonelier, flanked by snowposts. Yet that corner of Durham differs greatly from the landscape beyond Piercebridge. At Willington, for example, Dere Street enters a mining town. At Lanchester it meanders among slag heaps and second-hand car dumps. This is industrial Durham, a place where grass gives way to 'brass'. Marooned among it, I reflected that the case against industrial society rests on something stronger than a dislike of noise and a fondness for candle-light. Had I entered a Durham factory I would have met men who earned their living by performing a process that was certainly tedious and probably trivial. But had I entered a Durham farm I would have met men who at the end of each day could point to a well-tilled field, saying: 'That is *my* work'. Likewise a saddler makes a saddle, a carpenter makes a chair, a tailor makes a jacket. And they, too, can say: 'that is *my* work'. Machinery, on the other hand, has ensured that practically nothing is made by anyone in particular. One day, perhaps, society will impose a division of labour whereby the majority of people spend a season of every year in a factory, and another season in a field, and another season in a ship. Even an unskilled labourer will then discover that variety adds spice to life, according to the gospel of W. H. Davies:

When will it come, that golden time,
When every heart must sing?
The power to choose the work we love
Makes every man a king.

Dreary though they are, these outposts of industry cannot dim the high and wide hinterland of moors and hills and becks. In Lincolnshire, as we have seen, a traveller might think that he was still in East Anglia; nor would some parts of south Yorkshire persuade him that he was any further north than Derbyshire; but in County Durham he approaches the very peak of what is meant by the phrase 'North Country'. People who know that northern peak are sometimes at a loss to define it, even as Housman was at a loss to define poetry (except as a physical sensation). Partly, of course, the peak consists of accent and dialect, of climate and contours, of customs, crafts, industries, sports; and partly it consists of the men who made and were moulded by those things. On the not numerous occasions when Hilaire Belloc ventured north of Sussex, he under-estimated what he found:

> The men that live in North England
> I saw them for a day;
> Their hearts are set upon the waste fells,
> Their skies are fast and grey . . .

'Waste fells'? But those fells nurture the finest sheep in Britain. Grey skies? But that is a poetically unjust way of stating that some parts of the north receive less sunshine than do the south. The north is a man's country. When I was a child it was so much a man's country that women were neither expected nor indeed allowed to enter a village inn. The northern climate breeds a hardihood that is a matter of fact, not a flight of fancy. Except in the regimented industrial zones, the northerners are self-reliant. Wherever possible, they help themselves and one another rather than wait for strangers to effect a rescue. They are often blunt, sometimes brusque, occasionally surly; and that, too, is a response to their climate.

At Ebchester the old Dere Street entered *Vindomora*, a Roman camp, whose rubble went to build a Norman church. The marching songs of the Roman soldiers were ultimately replaced by the marching song of the Durham Light Infantry, 'The Light Barque'. Until many of them were either merged or disbanded, nearly every English regiment had its own marching song. In the north east the Lincolnshire Regiment chose 'The Lincolnshire

Poacher'; the East Yorkshire Regiment chose 'The Yorkshire Lass'; the Border Regiment chose 'D'ye Ken John Peel?'; the West Riding Regiment chose 'The Wellesley', commemorating its famous colonel, Arthur Wellesley, first Duke of Wellington.

In Ebchester a bridge across the River Derwent marked yet another county border, which yet another sudden squall obliterated. To the whine therefore of wind and rain I entered Northumberland, the largest of the Border counties, nowadays a peacefully prosperous county, though formerly a realm of

old, unhappy, far-off things,
And battles long ago.

6 THE BORDER COUNTRY

Northumberland is the most regal and the most rural of all the English counties. While Cornwall crawls with cars, and the Norfolk Broads are good for business and little else, still the Northumbrian lanes go their own way, and the North Sea suffers no speedboats. In June on The Cheviot I have enjoyed six hours of solitude that were made companionable by the sight of a shepherd and his dog, too distant to be hailed. In August near Kirkharle I have walked from noon till teatime without meeting a car. Industry confines itself to the south-east of the county, at Newcastle, Tynemouth, Blyth. The rest is sheep, cattle, crops, birds, waves, and in winter a wind:

On Keilder side the wind blows wide,
There sounds nae hunting horn
That rings sae sweet as the winds that beat
Round the banks where Tyne is born.

Southrons may suppose that Swinburne's 'nae' and 'sae' are Lowland Scots, as indeed they are, but only because Lowland Scots is Highland English, a dialect which crossed the border from Carlisle. Southrons may also suppose that the far north was always an uncouth land, peopled by illiterate peasants. But the truth is otherwise, for while King Alfred complained that scholarship in southern England had almost vanished, Northumbria was the home of Caedmon and Cuthbert and Bede. There dwelt the monks who excelled at preserving, copying, and creating literature; there the evangelists preached a gospel of *charitas* to an age of violence; and there, on its northern frontier, lurked the Scots, whose invasions spanned the centuries from Roman Emperor to Hanoverian King.

The entry into Northumberland offers no sudden change of

scene. Dere Street travels several miles before the country becomes gentler and more speckled with the streams which Northumbrians call 'burns'. Language, on the other hand, does change, both written and spoken, for a signpost points toward Broomhaugh, a Northumbrian name, *haugh*, meaning 'alluvial riverside land'. The accent differs too. Defoe cited an example: 'the natives of this county, of the ancient original race or families, are distinguished by . . . a difficulty in pronouncing the letter *r*, which they cannot deliver from their tongues without a hollow jarring sound in the throat . . . this they call the Northumbrian r . . .'. Some people regard the 'r' as an echo of Harry Hotspur's speech defect, which the Northumbrians copied, so fervently did they admire the warlike earl. There, perhaps, is an instance of what I have called a 'particular' source of local intonation. Until the end of the eighteenth century, almost every Englishman

Clifton Hampden, Oxfordshire

Here the stripling Thames flows among level meadows overlooked by Wittenham Clumps and the skyline Chilterns. Here lived a Poet Laureate of England, John Masefield OM, in a house whose lawns sloped to the river. Here, too, voyaged a famous trio, Jerome K. Jerome's *Three Men in a Boat* (not forgetting the dog, Montmorency). They found the Barley Mow 'the quaintest, most old-world inn up the river . . . Its low-pitched gables and thatched roof and lattice windows give it a story-book appearance . . .'.

Until 1864 the villagers crossed the Thames by ferry, but in that year a bridge of six redbrick arches was designed by Sir George Gilbert Scot, with a narrow pavement allowing pedestrians to avoid the toll which was levied on horsemen and vehicles. While the pleasure boats ply briskly, a walker may, like Edmund Spenser, stroll leisurely

Along the shore of silver-streaming Thames.

spoke the dialect of his region. Hotspur himself spoke what we would call broad Northumbrian; Sir Francis Drake spoke broad Devon; Nicholas Breakspear (the only English Pope) spoke Hertfordshire; Shakespeare spoke Warwickshire; an eighteenth-century squire, Sir Pitt Crawley of *Vanity Fair* 'spoke in the coarsest and vulgarest Hampshire accent'. Standard or King's English is an echo of London's prestige, which now attracts the heirs of men who, until the reign of George III, would have been content to prosper in York, or Bristol, or Norwich, and to send their sons to the same grammar school at which they themselves had been educated. Nevertheless, we are still left wondering why the Northumbrian 'r' is confined to certain areas of the county and why a Tyneside collier still uses words and intonations unlike those of his fellow-Northumbrians at Wooler.

Meanwhile, my entry into Northumberland was greeted by

Christ Church, Oxford

When Matthew Arnold's scholar gipsy was roaming the Oxfordshire countryside he

> Turn'd once to watch, while thick the snowflakes fall,
> The line of festal lights in Christ-Church hall . . .

Oxford men call this famous college 'The House', a version of its original name, *Aedes Christi* or 'Christ's House'. Founded in 1525 by Cardinal Wolsey, it was meant to outshine every other college in Christendom. Endowments provided for a dean, one hundred canons, sixteen choristers, thirteen chaplains, twelve clerks, six professors, and a music teacher. The tower was designed by Sir Christopher Wren. Its bell, Great Tom, still sounds curfew. Fame answers 'Adsumus' to the college roll call: Sir Philip Sidney, William Penn, John Wesley, John Ruskin, Lewis Carroll, and three eminent statesmen, Canning, Gladstone, and Sir Robert Peel (the first man to achieve a Double First).

another change of weather. The clouds dispersed, revealing once more a blue and brilliant sky. Every leaf and each flower had been rinsed by the recent rain. Indeed, the air was now so clear that, approaching Corbridge, I looked beyond the town, with the mind's eye seeing clearly those hills which to the physical eye were merely half-imagined smudges. A comparable vision befell an American blacksmith, Elihu Burritt, who in 1864 wrote *A Walk from London to John o'Groat's with Notes by the Way*. When Burritt reached Northumberland he perceived the numinous memories: 'This,' he exclaimed, 'is the Border-land! Here the fiercest antagonisms of hostile nationalities met in deadly conflict. Fire and blood, rapine and wrath blackened and ravaged for centuries across this bleak country'. An early relic of those wars can be seen at Corbridge, site of *Corsopitum*, a Roman fort, covering twenty-two acres. It can be seen again at Hadrian's Wall, stretching from a point near Bowness-on-Solway to the outskirts of Newcastle upon Tyne, a distance of eighty miles. The Wall was garrisoned by seventeen forts, some of which held a thousand troops. Between each fort stood a mile-castle, manned by fifty troops; and between each mile-castle stood a look-out post, manned by four troops. Only thrice in three centuries did the savages breach the Wall; and after each assault the breach was mended.

Rome, however, ventured far beyond Corbridge. In the Perthshire mountains she established outposts that kept an eye on the tribesmen. Service north of the Wall was regarded almost as a punishment. The climate, said the Romans, was so atrocious that only serpents and Scotsmen could long survive it. The land was bereft of anything which a Roman soldier would have rated as civilised. Just so, Kipling's 'Tommy Atkins' sweated and shivered on the Khyber Pass, harassed day and night by natives who glided like ghosts through their own terrain. Whenever I visit Hadrian's Wall I remember the words of William Camden written three centuries ago: 'Verily I have seen the tracts of it over the high pitches and steep decent of the hills: wonderfully rising and falling . . .'. Wonderfully indeed; a defence unique in Europe, built by men who imposed a veneer of civilisation on their barbarian subjects. And this they achieved because they were strong and unafraid, neither submitting to a show of hands nor treating their inferiors as equals. Their word was law: *Roma locuta est; causa finita est* ('Rome has spoken; that is that'). If Rome had not spoken, some of us might still be daubing our faces with woad.

At Hadrian's Wall three routes invited me to follow them: Dere Street, the Pennine Way, and the road to Rothbury. I had travelled them all many times, on foot and in a car. Rather than decline two invitations, I accepted three, continuing along Dere Street, which crossed the Wall at Portgate. Did the Romans glance back, I wondered, when they, too, marched north for Scotland, leaving behind them the Wall's comfort and security? Did they, too, feel the spell of a wild and savage countryside? Some of them never returned to answer, but were caught in a blizzard, or killed while they slept, not knowing that the Scots had crawled through the midnight heather, silently spearing the sentries.

West-north-west went Dere Street, often unfenced, always straight, never wide; growing steadily steeper and lonelier as it hugged the original course. The sheep that grazed there in Roman times were scraggy and small, unlike the plump Cheviots that now feed on the heights and beside the burns. The meaning of 'Cheviot' is unknown; its accepted pronunciation is 'Cheeviot'. Sometimes called the Great Sheep, Cheviots underwent selective breeding during the second half of the eighteenth century when an English farmer, named Robson, crossed some of his Northumbrian Long Hills with three rams from the Lincolnshire Wolds, to produce the flocks which soon afterwards crossed the border, and in 1792 reached Caithness. When Burritt cited 'the white wealth of their wool' his alliteration evoked both the symbol and the substance of England's medieval prosperity. Not without reason does the Lord Chancellor sit on a sack of wool in the House of Lords.

After several miles the modern road went its own way to Scotland via Carter Bar, leaving Dere Street to cross the Border near Newton St Boswells, sometimes as a grassy track, sometimes as an overgrown footpath, sometimes as a faint shadow, and sometimes as an invisible conjecture. I, too, forsook the modern road, not in order to follow Dere Street, but to revisit a lonely and unfenced lane leading to a mysterious village in a houseless country. During my first journey along that lane I had been astonished to find a small church alone on a knoll. Since our fathers did not set a church where none was needed, I assumed that Thockrington village must lie in a hollow on the far side of the knoll. But neither there nor anywhere else could I discover the village. The only buildings were one farm and one cottage. More than ever baffled, I entered the church, expecting to find it derelict. Not at all; it was clean and well preserved. Who worshipped there? Who had worshipped when it was built? I stared through the open doorway, as if seeking an answer, but heard only the silence. Yet the church itself contained the answer, printed on the back of a photograph. Founded by the Umbraville family in 1100, Thockrington church served a village which stood a little to the north-east, in the diocese of Durham. When one of the Umbravilles damaged some property belonging to the Archbishop of York, the church was forfeit to the See of York, and remained there for 625 years, whereafter it reverted to Durham. In 1847 a seafaring native returned to Thockrington, carrying the germs of cholera, which infected the whole village. Thockrington, in fact, was wiped out and never rebuilt.

On my second visit I examined the tombstones in that lonely churchyard, which appeared to be no more than a walled enclosure of part of the surrounding sheep-walk. Among those memorials I found one to the Shafto family, who had resided at Bavington Hall, a few miles north-east of Thockrington, until they lost their estate by supporting the Old Pretender. More than two centuries later, in 1953, Mr Robert Shafto returned to his ancestral home. An earlier Robert Shafto is remembered via the unrequited love that was felt for him by the daughter of a neighbour, Sir Henry Belayse of Brancepeth Castle:

> Bobby Shafto's gone to sea,
> With silver buckles on his knee;
> He'll come back and marry me,
> Bonnie Bobby Shafto.

And now, on my third visit, this vanished village and these houseless hills looked exactly the same as when I had first seen them. Even the grass looked the same; not a new herbage, reborn through many years, but the original turf, stretching toward infinite loneliness. That illusion soon faded, for the hills became less bare, and woods appeared, and after a few miles the lane entered Kirkharle, a hamlet among trees, birthplace of Lancelot Brown, nicknamed 'Capability' because of his flair for detecting the capability or potential of a garden. Starting as garden boy at Kirkharle Park, seat of the Loraine family, Brown climbed the ladder of English society. By hard work and natural ability he became the foremost landscape gardener of the eighteenth century, ending as High Sheriff of Huntingdonshire and Cambridgeshire, and father-in-law to Lord Holland. If you seek Brown's memorial, look at the gardens of Blenheim Palace and Syon House. The plinth in a meadow midway between Kirkharle Park and the church was erected by Brown's first master, Sir William Loraine, to commemorate an ancestor, Robert Loraine, 'barbarously murdered in this place by the Scots in 1483 for his services to his country against their thefts and robbery, as he was returning from the church alone, where he had been at his private devotions'. A later member of the family, Sir Percy Loraine, rendered 'his services to his country' as ambassador in Italy during the 1930s. Kirkharle is scarcely more than a row of neat cottages, each with a garden glowing as though 'Capability' himself were likely at any moment to revisit his old home.

'K to Cp beau as any in N 4 car 2 feet'. That cryptic entry in my notebook served to remind me that the lane from Stamfordham to Capheaton is as beautiful as any in Northumberland, and that I had travelled it four times by car and twice on foot. Capheaton is in some ways a feudal place and all the better for it. The cottages are as spick as span; their gardens dead-heat for first prize; the lanes look as though they were swept every morning. Capheaton Hall is the seat of the Swinburnes, who have resided there since it was built during the Restoration, at which time they acquired a baronetcy. The family's most famous member—son of an Admiral—was Algernon Charles Swinburne, a psychopathic genius, who mastered the art of English verse, but was sometimes less adroit in the choice of propositions which he propounded. Swinburne obeyed too literally his family motto, *Semel et Semper* or 'Always the Same'. In short, a part of his personality never grew up. Only in childhood and during Eton holidays did he stay at Capheaton. He was by temperament a Londoner, greatly awed by the majesty of Putney Heath. 'The first duty of a singer,' he declared, 'is to sing.' When that ancient maxim became unfashionable, Laurence Binyon looked beyond the vogue: 'It may be that with the reaction against the harsh matter and deflated rhythms there will come a revived enjoyment of Swinburne's clear and confident singing voice . . . in his own especial sphere he is supreme'. Swinburne was certainly 'clear and confident' when he echoed the Northumbrian scene:

> Through fell and moorland
> And salt-sea foreland
> Our noisy norland
> Resounds and rings . . .

Otterburn lies twelve miles north-west of Capheaton. The most impressive approach is via the lane from Bellingham (pronounced 'Bellinjam'), which crosses a moor and then the River Otter, from whose bridge you see a handsome stone building, a tweedmill, owned by the Waddell family, proving that a rural industry can blend with its landscape. Otterburn's old houses would look better without the company of their modern neighbours. The fame of this village is marked by two memorials: one, a plinth, stands in a coppice on the edge of the parish; the other, a seat, bears an inscription: 'In these fields . . . the Battle of Otterburn was fought and deeds were done which in the noblest of English ballads live immortally recorded'. Sometimes called the Battle of Chevy Chase, this once-famous encounter occurred in 1388, when the Scottish Earl of Douglas crossed the border, ravaged the countryside, insulted Sir Henry Percy, and was pursued by him. At Otterburn the Scots camped for the night, intending to waylay the English next day. Sure enough, the English arrived, weary after a long march. But instead of resting they went straight into a night action. Each side claimed a victory which neither achieved, for although Percy slew Douglas, he was himself taken prisoner. Few Englishmen nowadays have even heard of the battle; fewer still have read the ballad of *Chevy Chase*, though Addison called it 'the favourite ballad of the common people of England'.

The ballads came from both sides of the border. Most of them were anonymous, though some had been composed and handed down *viva voce* during the late Middle Ages. Many of the manuscript ballads were rescued from destruction by Bishop Percy, who collected and published them in 1765. Not every ballad is a war cry. Several are folk legends, or portraits of racy characters, or love stories:

I wish I were where Helen lies,
Night and day on me she cries;
O that I were where Helen lies,
On fair Kirconnell Lee!

How well I know that lane northward from Otterburn to Elsdon, a high and solitary hamlet, where a few cottages and one shop are set around a green dominated by the church and its former rectory or peel tower which the Borderfolk devised as a defence against the Scots. The word 'peel' comes from the Latin *palus*, meaning 'timber palisade'. The Borderers, however, built in stone, knowing that fire will easily destroy timber. In its simplest form the peel was a rectangular tower containing two or three storeys into which the villagers barricaded themselves and as many as possible of their livestock. The peel, in short, was a landbound Noah's Ark, designed to withstand arrows, bullets, spears, flames. The Elsdon farrier once told me that in his grandfather's day the rectory was still called 'The Castle'. Writing during the nineteenth century, Augustus Hare described Elsdon peel as 'a dismal old castle built to fortify the rector in moss-trooping times' ('moss-trooper' was first recorded in 1651, to connote the bandits who haunted the mossy Border). Enlarged by a Regency rector, Elsdon peel tower is now a layman's home, modernised within, yet preserving the appearance of a small fortress. Long after the Border wars had ceased, the Border country contained hundreds of peel parsonages. The last to go was at Chatton, where the tower served as the priest's house until 1834.

The lane out of Elsdon is steep and narrow. So far as I recall, you can walk northward along it for nearly two hours without reaching a crossroads. Some of the hills are wooded; others rise up like bald domes; all are grazed by Cheviots. Among those hills stands High Shaw, the home of a farmer who gave me a remarkable example of the regional Unconscious. At sunset in summer, he said, a few of the old farmers drive their livestock down from the summits. When asked to justify the move, they reply that at nightfall the grass in the valley becomes more succulent than the grass on the heights. It is useless to assure them that nightfall works no such miracle. They maintain the ritual because they are unconsciously repeating a custom of their forebears who, when dusk fell, gathered the animals close to the house lest the Scots came raiding.

This part of the Border is called Coquetdale, after the River Coquet, which flows through Rothbury, having risen in a wild region near Carter Bar, called Coquet Head (Old English *cocwudu* or 'forest of wild birds'). Rothbury itself is a little town of stone houses overlooking a steep street flanked by a grass verge and many trees. The street is called Rotten Row—a corruption of *route de roi*—because King John once followed it. Hills arise on all sides of Rothbury, crowned by Tosson, nearly fifteen hundred feet above the sea. Some of the oldest inhabitants are difficult to translate. Thus, when a ploughman asks his grandson to kick aside a large stone, he says: 'Gie yon gurt stane a cleep, wi' ye'.

Rothbury's famous man was William George Armstrong, son of a Newcastle corn merchant, who turned from law to engineering. His first major invention—a machine that generated frictional electricity—gained for him a Fellowship of the Royal Society when he was only thirty years old. Sometime later, dismayed by the ineffectiveness of English gunfire during the Crimean War, he invented a weapon more accurate than the current Army type. He then presented all patent rights to the nation. Knighted, he became Engineer of Rifle Ordnance. Ennobled as Lord Armstrong, he settled at Cragside, an estate on the edge of Rothbury, where he converted the house into a mansion. Today the Cragside gardens are open to the public during spring and summer. In them, while the sun shone, I gauged again the pace at which an English spring travels north, for although the Rothbury rhododendrons were only beginning to bloom, the Cornish ones had long since passed their prime. All Englishmen welcome the spring, but in Northumberland they grasp it with a gratitude deepened by the cold climate.

A dramatic change of scene occurs beyond Rothbury. Up goes the road, down come the gears, and the meadows give way to moorland. Only the sheep thrive, squelching through peat and reed. However, the barrenness is soon supplanted by fertile pastures. Eastward lies Alnwick Castle, seat of the north country's premier nobleman, the Duke of Northumberland, a descendant through the female line of the Earls of Northumberland. Medieval noblemen usually took their titles from a region in which they owned large estates; but in the eighteenth century, when many peerages were granted to the professional and merchantile classes, most of the *nouveaux riches* lacked an ancient territorial allegiance. Voltaire noted this fact in his *Lettres sur les Anglais*: 'very few of them have estates in those places whence they take their titles. One shall be the Duke of Dorsetshire, though he has not a foot in Dorsetshire; and another is the Earl of a village, though he scarce knows where it is situated'. The old tension and harmony between King and Lords and Commons bore little resemblance to the present balance of power, which has been tilted by universal suffrage, and now leans heavily in favour of any extra-parliamentary organisation strong enough to blackmail the whole kingdom. Many Englishmen believe that the House of Lords ought to be replaced by a Senate whose membership is neither ennobled nor hereditary. Such an arrangement would achieve two good things: first, it would put an end to the farce that now confers titles on people who have spent a lifetime trying to abolish titles; second, it would foster a true nobility by enabling the Sovereign now and again to award an hereditary title to persons who could properly support it.

On the road to Wooler, only a few miles from the sea, I noticed that the fields wore the level look which often marks a coastal hinterland. Westward, however, the Cheviot Hills stood like a treeless rampart, topped by The Cheviot, Northumberland's highest point, 2,676 feet among the larks. Solitude being partly a subjective state, gregarious visitors find the Wooler road a lonely one, though to countryfolk the wayside farms appear companionable. About eight miles short of Wooler, a lane leads westward to Ingram, passing a farmhouse and some cottages, and then delving among unoccupied hills. At the very moment when Ingram seems not to exist, the lane reaches an ugly modern bridge across the River Breamish, from which you see a church tower and several chimneys half-hidden by trees. I forget how many houses constitute the 'village centre'; four, perhaps. Ingram contains two heirlooms: first, its name, *Angr*, meaning 'grassland'; second, some arrow-slits in the church wall, a defence against the Scots. The manor house stands within a few yards of the church, and for several decades has lacked a resident seigneur. Although Ingram escaped the fate of Thockrington, it was destined to join those other settlements which shrivelled when technology decimated the number of farmfolk who dwelt there. Ingram's liveliest house is the home of Mr John Hope, Warden of the Northumberland National Park, who has several times taken me on safari in his Land-Rover, watching deer, spotting birds, meeting foresters.

What *is* a National Park? Part of the answer must be negative; in other words, a National Park is *not* a Nationalised Park. It is an area wherein certain landowners have granted specific access. The Countryside Commission underlines that point: 'Visitors,' it says, 'have no right of entry to private land or property; the farmer's fields remain private inside the National Parks, just as they are everywhere else'. In 1977 England and Wales contained ten such Parks: Peak District, Lakeland, Dartmoor, Exmoor, North Yorkshire, Yorkshire Dales, Northumberland, Snowdonia, Pembrokeshire, Brecon Beacons. Covering more than 5,000,000 acres or nine per cent of the area of England and Wales, the Parks are administered by the County Councils of the region in which they lie. But there is no guarantee that commerce will not be allowed to 'develop' these areas of 'outstanding natural beauty'. Speaking as Chairman of the National Parks Commission, Lord Strang admitted: 'Where a government department has had plans for erecting large installations of one kind or another in a National Park I can remember no case where it has been diverted from its purpose by anything the Commission might say about the intentions of Parliament as embodied in the National Parks Act'.

According to the Countryside Commission, the purpose of a National Park is 'to ensure that the control of development shall be conducted with special regard to the preservation and enhancement of its natural beauty and the promotion of facilities for open air recreation'. To protect the countryside against debasement is one thing; to convert it into a playground is another. Whenever tens of thousands of people are gathered together in the midst of beauty, they destroy the thing they came to see. On my first visit to Ingram the lane thither was known only to the local people; on my last visit the lane was littered with cars. Nor is Ingram the only victim. In 1972 the Friends of Lakeland reported that visitors to the Lakeland National Park were wearing away the surface of Helvellyn, England's third highest mountain. In 1973 the Chiltern Society reported that motorists were doing the same to Ivinghoe Beacon. In 1976 a section of the Peak District National Park was closed because visitors were setting fire to it. In the same year a National Parks survey showed that nearly seventy-five per cent of the motorists who visited Dartmoor walked less than one mile from their parked vehicle; nearly fifty per cent stayed within one hundred yards of it; and thirteen per cent never emerged from it. 'The last thing we want to see,' said the survey, 'is great concrete car parks ... People must be discouraged from taking their cars over the Moor.'

The further you go from London, the closer you come to England; and never closer than on the road to Wooler, studded with small woods and trim farmsteads. Almost everyone you meet earns his livelihood either by working on the land or by serving those who do work on it. Wooler itself stands astride a hill above Wooler Water. Glancing up at the sheep-walked skyline, a stranger might assume that Wooler's name is a synonym for 'wool town'. In fact, the name comes from *Wulloure* or 'banks of a stream'. By southern standards the town is no more than a village, yet it has held a sheep market since 1199. In 1968 or thereabouts I met Wooler's oldest inhabitant, a retired shepherd, nearly one hundred years of age, who remembered the annual hiring fair at which the farmers engaged their hinds and milk-maids for the next twelve month. The shepherd's recollections need to be translated: 'Th' auldsteers weird yan smocks' ('The old men wore smocks') ... 'A maid an' twa trugged th'auld peeal' ('One or two of the girls carried a pail') ... 'Hemmels weer hotchin' wi' haytimers' ('Some of the haymakers slept in an

117

open shed') . . . 'Mort o' maids an' braw lads bided wi' faymeer' ('Most of the girls and youths lodged with the farmer').

Wooler stands close to a hill called variously Hamildon, Humbleton, Holmedon. There a Border battle occurred in 1402. Who could have guessed that this remote place would one day be mentioned by Shakespeare?

> Young Harry Percy and brave Archibald,
> That ever-valiant and approvèd Scot,
> At Holmedon met . . .

But Wooler is linked with another and more momentous event, for in the town you may see the house at which the Earl of Surrey slept, on the eve of Flodden, the *locus classicus* of all Border battles. In 1513 King James IV of Scotland planned to attack England despite the fact that he had lately signed a treaty of perpetual friendship with the English King, Henry VIII, his own brother-in-law. While Henry and the Court were in France, James crossed the border with a large army, razing the castles of Wark, Norham, and Etel. At Ford, a few miles from Wooler, James became the self-invited guest of Lady Heron. On leaving, he repaid his hostess by burning her castle. But the English were not idle. When news of the invasion reached London, Queen Katherine ordered the Earl of Surrey to march north. Early in September the English army reached Wooler, less than a dozen miles from the Scots, who had encamped on high ground at Flodden. Surrey's son, Admiral Thomas Howard, devised a daring plan of attack whereby the English, having bypassed Flodden, would then turn west, so placing themselves between the Scots and Scotland. In order to achieve their purpose the English had first to cross the River Twill at Twizel Bridge, which they did unnoticed by the Scottish scouts. This manoeuvre was especially daring because the English were outnumbered two-to-one, and their food and ammunition had run low. Moreover, the Scots held a position that could be attacked only by climbing up to it. In theory, therefore, the Scots ought to have won an easy victory; in practice, they suffered a disastrous defeat. The fault was largely their own, for when the English had at last been sighted, James came down to meet them, instead of compelling them to scale his own hilltop position. So, in the end, each side faced its homeland. The nucleus of the Scottish army was the royal standard, defended by the King and his personal bodyguard. All around were the traditional Scottish shiltrons or circles of spears. But the English axemen hacked off the Scottish spearheads; their archers confirmed an international renown; their cavalry routed the remnant. Only the Scottish centre held, completely surrounded. Not King Harold's house-carles at Battle fought more gallantly than King James's bodyguard at Flodden. The King himself set the example, dying alongside his standard. Around him, when dusk fell, lay thirteen of his earls, three of his bishops, the flower of his gentry, and ten thousand other soldiers. Black Friday, as it came to be called, bequeathed to Scotland an infant King, a pawn in the hands of nobles who harried the land with their private feuds. The Border ballads uttered a famous pibroch for Flodden Field:

We'll hear nae mair lilting at our ewes milking,
Women and bairns are heartless and wae,
Singing and moaning on ilka green loaning,
The flowers of the forest are a'wede away.

Tudor chroniclers referred to Flodden as the Battle of Branxton because it occurred within sight of Branxton, a hamlet beside the road to Wooler, in whose church the body of King James was placed. When Beatrix Potter visited Flodden Field she found that the site of the battle was disputed. Her *Journal* for 25 July 1894 states: 'Drove to Flodden ... local difference of opinion as to spot, but pretty clear that no such thing as Flodden Field ... Papa had an argument with an old woman, who averred that the whole thing took place on Piper's Hill ...'. On a lane a few hundred yards west of Branxton, a decrepit gate leads to a steep footpath and thence to the summit of Piper's Hill, a green mound in an ocean of green hills. There, protected by iron railings, stands a plain granite cross, erected by the Scots in 1910. Nothing could be simpler nor more chivalrous than the inscription: *To the Brave of Both Nations. 1513.* Once a year, in August, a troop of Scots ride across the Border from Coldstream, to lay a wreath at the foot of the cross, whereafter they climb Branxton Hill, there to hold a service in memory of those who died in the battle. 'All of us who have a living capacity for emotion,' wrote Rudolf Otto, 'must at some time have known what it is like to have a feeling of eerieness.' Viewed solely as a landscape, Flodden Field is not at all eerie. On the contrary, it is peaceful and pastoral. But when viewed through the eyes of history it does become eerie. Even on a bright spring morning you listen for the thud of hooves, the clash of swords, the swish of arrows, the cry of pain. Flodden Field enshrines the dark aspects of the history of two kingdoms which, as Scott observed, regarded each other with an inbred hostility:

> By mutual inroads, mutual blows,
> By habit, and by nation, foes . . .

Forty years after the battle, the English and Scottish border wardens designated a No Man's Land, four miles wide and ten miles long, stretching from Langholm to Gretna Green. A joint proclamation declared: 'All English men and Scottish men, after this proclamation is made, are all and shall be free to rob, burn, spoil, slay, murder, and destroy all and every such person or persons, their bodies, buildings, goods, and cattle as do remain or shall inhabit upon any land of the said Debatable land, without any redress be made for same'.

The fruitful aspects of that warlike history are visible on the road to Cornhill, a dignified village, headquarters of the North Northumberland Foxhounds. The local inn, the Collingwood Arms, recalls that Lilburn Tower has been the seat of the Collingwood family since 1793. Northumberland, indeed, is strewn with memorials to that family's foremost member, Vice-Admiral Lord Collingwood. At Tynemouth are four of the cannon from his ship, *Royal Sovereign*, with a plaque: 'This monument was erected in 1845 by public subscription to the memory of Admiral Lord Collingwood who in the Royal Sovereign on the 21st October 1805 led the British fleet into action at Trafalgar and sustained the sea fight for upwards of an hour before the other ships were within gun-shot, which caused Nelson to exclaim: "See how that noble fellow Collingwood takes his ships into action!"'. At Matfen, where Collingwood's father-in-law lived, is a double-headed Spanish shot which struck the *Royal Sovereign*. At Morpeth is Collingwood House, where the Admiral lived with his family during the few brief intervals from sea service ('whenever I think how to be happy again,' he wrote, 'my thoughts carry me back to Morpeth'). In Newcastle Cathedral a memorial recalls that there he was baptised and married (ultimately to rest alongside Nelson in St Paul's Cathedral). In the same city, a monument on the old Quayside marks the site of his birthplace, and Trinity House contains a replica of the last ship he commanded. But no one will ever count the monuments raised by Collingwood himself when he scattered acorns that became the warships which David Garrick called 'Hearts of Oak'.

At the northern edge of Cornhill I reached the Scottish border, marked by John Smeaton's graceful five-arched bridge across the River Tweed, beyond which the roofs of Coldstream were seen. In 1926 the Coldstream Burns Club erected a plaque on the bridge: 'Robert Burns crossed this bridge entering England for the first time 7th May 1787, and kneeling prayed for a blessing on his native land:

O Scotia! my dear, my native soil!
For whom my warmest wish to Heaven is sent!
Long may thy hardy sons of rustic toil
Be blest with health, and peace and sweet content!'

Midway across the bridge I stood with one foot in Roxburghshire, the countryside of Lord Home, who resigned an ancient earldom in order to serve as prime minister in the Lower House. Down in Kent, you remember, the border with Sussex revealed no deep difference of dialect and tradition; but up in Roxburghshire the border led at once into another nation, for whereas the English were a predominantly Saxon people, the Scots retained much of their Celtic or Irish lineage, together with their own language, the Gaelic; their own form of Christianity, the Calvinist Kirk; their own form of law, with a verdict of Not Proven. Charles Lamb, that gentlest of Englishmen, confessed: 'I have been trying all my life to like Scotchmen, and am obliged to desist from the experiment'. Had Lamb crossed the Border into Coldstream, he would have concluded his experiment swiftly and successfully, not least because, like every other small Scottish town, Coldstream offers a spruceness and a welcome which few English towns now achieve.

Here, on the bridge, I reached my journey's furthest point from London, nearly three hundred-and-forty miles; to our great-great-grandfathers an unimaginable distance, though to our 'jet set' a mere half-hour's jaunt, just long enough to read the newspaper. Fortunately, however, gin-and-jets had scarcely touched this quiet corner of the kingdom. If Time had allowed, I could have met with people who in their childhood were in some ways closer to Stuart Scotland than to Welfare England. Many of them had neither visited nor desired to visit London. They lived at home among their crops and their beasts. Their capital was Edinburgh, or Berwick-on-Tweed. In my childhood the Scottish farmers had never seen a tractor. On the eve of World War II one of them told me that he would refuse to employ such a vehicle. 'They make a mort o' stink,' he said, 'and ne'er a mickle o' dung. Twa hoots an' they break doon. I'll be deed afore

Ribblesdale, Yorkshire

It seems strange that some of the loftiest land in England should be called dales, because 'dale' comes from an Old Germanic word, *dalon*, meaning 'low-lying place'. Evidently our forefathers chose to emphasise the depth of the valleys rather than the height of the hills.

There is a railway station at Horton-in-Ribblesdale, not far from the source of the River Ribble. The stationmaster was formerly required to send an hourly coded weather report to Dishford airport near York whence the news went to the Air Ministry in London. During the 1950s the Vicar of Ingleton held a monthly Evensong at Horton station. In that remote village King Henry VI was captured while hiding during the Wars of the Roses.

Ribblesdale is a rugged region, generally too high and wild for wheat, yet affording rich pastures for such hardy grazers as Herdwicks and Cheviots. Through it strides the Pennine Way, a public footpath stretching from Edale in Derbyshire to Kirk Yetholm in Roxburghshire.

a motor comes creeping o'er ma' own ferm.' Such an attitude may have been wrong, yet it existed and is therefore a relevant aspect of recent history.

On the bridge at Coldstream I greeted from after those many Northumbrian villages which Time and Space had set beyond my reach ... old friends such as Blanchland, Gilsland, Lanercost, Haltwhistle, Bellingham, and Holy Island, that speak of saintly rock, the haven of Aidan and Cuthbert. The most I could do was to revisit Byrness, a new village on an old site, built especially for men of the Forestry Commission, topped by craggy heights, slashed by regimented conifers, in winter covered with snow. Here the scenery is almost Norwegian, watered by white cascades that resemble little fjords, and dominated by summits whose conifers propound a curveless geometry. At Byrness I walked a short distance along the Pennine Way, which I once

Castlerigg, Cumbria

Forming an oval, these thirty-eight Celtic stones, known as The Carles, stand beside a path from Goosewell to Castlerigg, two miles east of Keswick. A line drawn across the two highest stones, and then aligned north and south, passes directly over the summits of Skiddaw and Helvellyn. In short, this is a prehistoric temple.

Most scholars believe that the stones were raised by Druids, a word first recorded in 1563, supposedly from a Celtic root, meaning 'magician or soothsayer'. Caesar described the Druids as a priestly caste, exempt from taxation and military service. They never committed their beliefs to writing, but handed them down *viva voce* to the initiates. Lucan, a late Latin writer, summarised the Druidic creed: 'The same spirit has a body again elsewhere, and death is but a midpoint in long life'. Druids survived in the Isle of Man until the fifth century AD, still making a sacrifice of living human beings.

125

followed from its southern terminus at Edale in Derbyshire to its northern terminus at Kirk Yetholm in Roxburghshire, a stroll of two hundred-and-fifty miles along the windswept spine of the north country.

Finally I returned to my allotted task, travelling south-west through forest, farmland, moorland; anciently a region of murder and pillage, but now as peaceful as when Sir Walter Scott praised it:

Sweet Teviot! on thy silver tide
The glaring bale-fires blaze no more;
No longer steel-clad warriors ride
Along thy wild and willow'd shore;
Where'er thou wind'st, by dale or hill,
All, all is peaceful, all is still . . .

Was that stillness a lull before the storm? At the beginning of the twentieth century it would have seemed inconceivable that Scotland should ever wish to disrupt the United Kingdom and to become yet another tiny republic whose defence and livelihood depend on a powerful neighbour. But now at last the impossibility is almost a probability. Shall I live to see a kilted ambassador at the Disunited Nations, and a Scottish President touting for votes, and the hardy Highlanders wallowing in an oily Scottish Ocean?

7 LAKELAND

Fore-and-aft the motionless cars sweated in sunlight, their tinware stabbing the eye. Fingers tapped impatient steering wheels. Children grizzled. Women yawned. Dogs panted. Suddenly the crocodile jerked forward a few yards, then wavered, creaked, and once more halted. Such was my progress along the main roads of Lakeland. At Windermere the water whined with speedboats and transistors. At Ambleside the crowds queued to cross the street. At Troutbeck they looked down on a garish encampment of tents and caravans. Wordsworth detected the earliest symptoms of the disease nearly two centuries ago: 'no one,' he wrote, 'can now travel through the more unfrequented tracts, without being offended, at almost every turn, by an introduction of discordant objects . . .'. In short, there are two Lakelands, identical yet different. One of them is Lakeland on any fine day between April and October; the other is Lakeland on most weekdays between October and April.

First recorded in 1829, the word 'Lakeland' connotes parts of the ancient counties of Lancashire, Westmorland, and Northumberland. The word 'Lancashire' comes from the county town, Lancaster or *Lancastra*, meaning 'Roman fort on the River Lune'. The word 'Westmorland' comes from *Westmoringaland*, meaning 'the land of the *Westmoringas*' (who lived west of the Yorkshire moors). The word 'Cumberland' comes from *Cymry*, meaning 'The Welsh' (Cumberland was formerly part of the Celtic kingdom of Strathclyde).

How large is Lakeland? What are its boundaries? W G. Collingwood described it as the mountainous country within fifteen miles of Grasmere; but that excludes many places that are commonly regarded as lying within Lakeland. A wider description was offered by Professor Sir Albert Seward: 'The

English Lake District, an approximately circular area 35 miles in diameter in the counties of Cumberland and Westmorland ...'. But that excludes the Lancashire lakes and mountains. Seward, however, added a postscript: 'even a superficial knowledge of its geological history can hardly fail to supplement a purely aesthetic enjoyment ...'. Coming from a geologist, that was a modest estimate of the relevance of his own studies. Nowhere in England are the effects of climate and earthquake more dramatic than in Lakeland. The oldest rocks are the Skiddaw Slates; most of the others are either Silurian or Ordovician. The Silurian rocks, which predominate in the southern half of the district, were named after the Silures, a Marcher tribe who defied the Romans. The Ordovician rocks, which predominate in the northern half, were named after the Ordovices, another Marcher tribe, the last to yield to Rome. Since the nomenclature of geology is uniform throughout the world, several types of rocks bear names that were bestowed by British geologists, notably William Smith, Adam Sedgwick, and Roderick Murchison.

The youngest Lakeland rocks—perhaps three thousand million years old—are red sandstone, as in the Furness and Eden areas. Earthquakes and glaciers occurred so long ago, and were so violent, that they tax the imagination. We feel more at ease when considering their effects on our food, houses, clothes, crafts, customs, industries, temperaments. Thus, few medieval Rutlanders ever saw a ship; few medieval Cornishmen built a timber house; few medieval Oxonians entered a tin mine; few medieval Devonians burned coal. Rocks still condition much of our economy, for the Durham collier plies a trade that seems as strange to a Norfolk thatcher as the thatcher's seems to a Kentish maltster. All those variations are byproducts of earthquake and erosion.

I approached Lakeland from Carlisle, capital of the English border region. If you enter from the south you are greeted by industrial estates; if from the north, by skyscraping offices. North, therefore, or south, the scene is much the same as those on the outskirts of most other large English towns. Dwarfed by commercial consortia, the nucleus of Carlisle contains a red sandstone church which became a cathedral in 1139, and was enlarged at intervals until 1362. Carlisle Castle was begun by

William II of England; was completed by David I of Scotland when he captured the city; and was again seized by the Scots in 1745. The seventeenth-century Tullie House and the eighteenth-century town hall differ somewhat from the twentieth-century civic centre. The city's handsomest houses—in English Street, Lowther Street, and Victoria Place—reflect a dour good taste.

At Penrith the traffic from the north met the traffic from the south, and together we crawled into Lakeland. Once again, therefore, I relieved the tedium by indulging a revierie, this time about William Wordsworth, who was born at Cockermouth in Cumberland, and spent most of this life near Grasmere in Westmorland. The Lake District, said Wordsworth, 'is a sort of national property, in which every man has a right and interest who has an eye to perceive and a heart to enjoy'. Posterity has rewritten that declaration as follows: 'The Lake District is a sort of national property, in which every man has a right and interest to drive a car, acquire a weekend cottage, perpetrate motorways, petrol pumps, caravan sites, lucky charm shops, fish-and-chipperies, Bingo bars, and car parks'. Nothing imaginable can grant Lakeland a happy issue out of those afflictions, because nothing imaginable can reduce the number of visitors who smother Lakeland's true identity as defined by Dorothy Wordsworth: 'not Man's hills, but all for themselves, the sky and the clouds, and a few wild creatures'. Nothing, then, can cure the disease; but the pain would be eased, and the proliferation checked, if tourists' cars were banned from selected areas, leaving the traveller to proceed either on foot or by public transport.

At Keswick a broken-down lorry blocked the narrow street, as though to recall Wordsworth's protest against the coming of the railway to Windermere:

Is there no nook of English ground secure
From rash assault?

During the hold-up my thoughts returned to Wordsworth and his guide book to Lakeland, the best of its kind yet written. It first appeared as an anonymous preface to a friend's illustrated travelogue. More than twenty years later the preface was expanded and published separately under a resounding title:

*A Guide Through The District Of The Lakes In The North of England
with a Description of the Scenery, etc., for the use of Tourists and Residents.*
In that book Wordsworth delivers his verdict on the Lakeland
scene as it appeared to a Lakelander who had walked through
Switzerland, Germany, and France: 'I do not indeed know of
any tract of country in which, within so narrow a compass, may
be found an equal variety of the influence of light and shadows
upon the sublime or beautiful features of landscape'. What of
Scotland and Wales? Wordsworth acknowledges their
attractions, but cites their flaws: 'in Scotland, particularly, what
long tracts of desolate country intervene· so that the traveller,
when he reaches a spot deservedly of great celebrity, would find
it difficult to determine how much pleasure is owing to
excellence inherent in the landscape itself; and how much to an
instantaneous recovery from oppression left upon his spirits by
the barrenness and desolation through which he has passed'.
Amen to that, will say the man who has walked across Rannoch
Moor. At what season does Lakeland reach the peak of
perfection? Wordsworth answers: 'About the first week in
October . . . the brilliant and various colours of the fern are then
in harmony with the autumnal woods . . .'. Cynics will protest
that the first week in October (and the other three also) are likely
to be wet and therefore a wash-out. Wordsworth replies: 'The
country is, indeed, subject to much bad weather . . . but the
number of black drizzling days, that blot out the face of things, is
by no means *proportionally* great'.

At last the lorry lumbered forward, followed by the queue of
sedentary sightseers. I turned into a cart track, to let the cortège
pass by. Then I followed my own devious route north-west to
Ennerdale Water, formerly called Ehen Lake, after a Viking
chief, *Ehen*. This lake is certainly the remotest and possibly the
wildest in England. Beyond it and all around rise gaunt cliffs,
scarred by aeons of rain and frost and sun; and above those
heights others appear, more distant, more daunting. There is
nothing gentle at Ennerdale, nothing hospitable; neither
prettiness nor charm. But majesty abounds there, pressed down
and overflowing from the shores to the summits. Austere, aweful,
sublime; Ennerdale is a place where those words retain their true
meaning. From the summit of Pillar Rock I boxed a rugged

compass, half-consciously seeking replies to questions which I alone could answer. Ought I to revisit St Bees and its seaside abbey and venerable school? Ought I to revisit Buttermere and Crummock Water, surely the loveliest of the lakes? Ought I to climb Skiddaw, the roof of England, more than three thousand feet above the sea? Ought I to call on the Bassenthwaite shepherd who, sixty years ago, won the pole jump at Grasmere sports? Could I ignore Furness Abbey, whose ruined silhouette resembled 'a rose-red city, half as old as Time'? Could I shun Saddleback and the green Vale of St John, happy hunting ground of my famous namesake and of the present Blencathra Pack? What of Borrowdale, Esk Hause, Helvellyn, Ullswater?

Trusting rather to memory than to maps, I headed south for Wrynose Pass and the Three Shires Stone that marks the meeting of Westmorland, Cumberland, and Lancashire. Is Wrynose more majestic than Ennerdale? Who knows? Who cares? Like Oxford and Cambridge, true majesty needs not contend for precedence. It is enough to say that at Wrynose Pass the world is ringed with rocks resembling the ramparts of a castle so ancient that only the aeons were able to erode them. Far below, a valley twists among interlocking spurs. House, church, barn, byre . . . none exists to be seen. It is, in Wordsworth's phrase, a land

Where, save the rugged road, we find
No appanage of human kind;
Nor hint of man . . .

The natives are sheep, rabbits, stoats, birds, wind, rain, and occasionally the sun; all else being intrusions. Even the Romans must have felt awed while they hacked part of this road as a highway from Ambleside to the coast via Hardknott Castle, their mountainous fortress.

One visit to the Lakeland mountains is not enough, nor a dozen returns. You must come by day and at night, in youth and in age, through sunshine and snow. Yet a thousand such journeys will miss their mark unless you get out and walk and climb; and even then you will fail to arrive unless you halt and ask and listen; and even the keenest ear and the canniest question will learn no more than a thousandth part of the shepherd's lifelong lesson; and not even the shepherd lives long enough to parse more than a few pages of an infinite library. Perhaps only the mountains are beginning to get the feel of the place.

Somewhere in this wilderness a spring begets the River Duddon, praised by Wordsworth with thirty-four sonnets, a tribute unique in literature:

> Pure flow the verse, pure, vigorous, and free,
> For Duddon, long-loved Duddon, is my theme!

At Cockley Bridge a lonely farmhouse appears, whereafter the river and the lane meander through meadows between mountains, but not for long. Swerving past another farmhouse (nowadays a hostel), the lane begins to climb, the river starts to race, and the mountains close in. After a mile or so the river encounters several waterfalls that sprinkle the grass beside the lane. In winter and early spring the banks of the Duddon are seldom disturbed by anything louder than a grazing Herdwick. If a car does pass, you do not hear it above the waterfalls.

At Seathwaite the lane squeezes itself between a church and a house, a feat which not every motorist performs unscathed. Then it passes an inn and a few farms and cottages, all cupped in a valley crowned by sheep-walk summits. Here lived Wordsworth's friend, Robert Walker, whom Lakelanders remember as 'Wonderful' Walker. Born at Seathwaite in 1707, one of a family of twelve, Walker was so frail that his parents doubted he would ever be able to earn his living as a hind. Despite their poverty, therefore, they paid a penny or two each week, that he might learn to read and write at a dame school in the village church. The child repaid them amply. As a schoolmaster at Loweswater he taught himself Latin and Greek. Returning to Seathwaite, he served the parish as curate for sixty-six years, starting with a weekly stipend of about eight new pence. He married a local maidservant, raised eight healthy children (one of whom became a priest), and, by renting a few acres, increased his weekly stipend to thirty new pence. He sheared his own sheep, made his own honey, tanned the hides of his own cattle, and helped his wife to make clothes and boots for the family. In the depths of winter he crossed Wrynose on foot, carrying wool and other produce to Ambleside market. Like the rest of his flock, he helped the neighbours at lambing, shearing, dipping, haytiming. He nursed them when they were sick, mixing medicines from his herb garden. He wrote their letters and legal documents. He taught their children in the church where he had himself been taught, using the altar as a desk. Although his family ate meat only once a week, neither friend nor stranger went empty away from his cottage. And when he died, at the age of ninety-two, he had managed to save £2,000, which in those years was a not-so-small fortune. Walker's church has vanished despite Ruskin's effort to repair and preserve it. The present church is small and plain. Its parish register contains this entry: 'Buried, June 28th, the Rev. Robert Walker. He was curate of Seathwaite for sixty-six years. He was a man singular for his temperance, industry, and integrity.' As Wordsworth remarked in another context: 'Brief notices of his life ought to find a place in the History . . .'.

From Seathwaite the Duddon trips and tumbles and sometimes leaps in its eagerness to reach the sea. At the next hamlet, Ulpha, the river swirls within a few yards of a whitewashed church with a bell-turret in place of a tower. There you will find the Arms of Queen Anne, some medieval roof timbers, and a pair of handcuffs that were used in years when the sexton was *ex officio* constable. Time has not outdated Wordsworth's description of the Lakeland churches: 'They exhibit generally a well-proportioned oblong, with a suitable porch, in some instances a steeple tower, and in others nothing more than a small belfry . . . how small must be the congregation there assembled, as it were, like one family; and proclaiming at the same time the depth of that seclusion in which the people live . . .'.

Ulpha is about as small as Seathwaite. It includes a bridge, a telephone box, a few farms and cottages, and a vicarage in whose riverside garden I used to sun myself with the priest and his wife and their brood of barefoot children. At Ulpha the lane still rises and falls alongside the spritely Duddon; but after a few miles the river passes from prime to age and thence into a Lancashire estuary.

It is possible to explore a large part of Lakeland without

venturing more than a few miles along the main roads. You require only leisure and the ability to read a map. My own journey from Ulpha to Helvellyn passed through Grizebrook, Thwaite Head, and the Devil's Gallop which, although they were in Lancashire, bore little resemblance to Wigan, Burnley, Rochdale, Nelson. I sighted Coniston Water and Ruskin's old home, Brantwood. I lingered at Hawkshead, a maze of alleys and cottages, where Wordsworth was schooled. I called at Sawrey, where Beatrix Potter, having become Mrs William Heelis, turned from rabbits to sheep, and was elected chairman of England's most masculine club, the Herdwick Sheep-Breeders' Association (imagine the Pope being elected Moderator of the Free Kirk of Scotland). Keeping strictly to the bylanes, I passed through a terrain which retained many of the features noted by William Camden in 1586: 'the mountains standing thick together, rich of mettal mines, and betweene them great meeres stored with all kinds of wild fowls . . . pretty hills for good pasturage and well replenished with flocks of sheep, beneath which again you meet with goodly plaines spreading out a great way, yielding corne sufficiently'. Celia Fiennes was less favourably impressed: 'they have only the summer graine as barley oates peas and lentils no wheate or rhye, for they are so cold and late in their yeares . . .'. The roads, she added, were neither fast nor numerous: 'these stony hills and wayes pulls of a shoe and wears them as thinn that it was a constant charge to shooe my horses every 2 or 3 days . . .'. Modern tourists are no longer delayed by the need to admire the landscape. While a wide race track at the foot of Helvellyn enables them to arrive without noticing the mountain, a motorway on the other side of Westmorland enables them to traverse the majestic Tebay Gorge so swiftly that the whole business is over in a couple of minutes. This invasion by tourists, however, was launched long before cars were invented. The name 'Laker' or 'visitor to Lakeland' was first recorded in 1798; and the rise of the Lakeland tourist trade can be traced with fair accuracy via Dorothy Wordsworth's *Journal* for 1803, which recalls a time when parts of Kent were 'as retired and as little known to travellers as our own Cumberland mountain wilds 30 years ago'. Wordsworth described the early 'Lakers' as 'Persons of taste, and feeling for

Landscape'. But when the railway reached Windermere, he castigated those who turned a blind eye on a future which they did not wish to see. Harriet Martineau, an early exponent of unfeminine feminism, declared: 'We have no fear of either the moral or commercial mischief in the region from the opening of the railway to it'. Canute's councillors, you remember, placed a similar trust in the waves. One wishes that Miss Martineau could see Windermere today.

By devious lanes, then, I reached Helvellyn, England's third highest mountain, partly in Westmorland and partly in Cumberland. My first ascent, many years ago, began from Wythburn's whitewashed church on the banks of Thirlmere. My last ascent began from Patterdale, where I joined the queue of fellow-climbers on a relatively easy track to the summit. The only awkward interlude occurs at Striding Edge, a narrow fairway between two precipices. In summer it all seems simple; in winter, however, the Lakeland rescue teams risk their lives trying to retrieve a halfwit who climbed during a mist, wearing plimsoles. On that point at least, Harriet Martineau's *Complete Guide* came down to earth: 'Once for all let us say, in all earnestness, and with the most deliberate decision, that no kind of tourist should ever cross the higher passes, or ascend the mountains, without a guide'.

Not far from Striding Edge you will see a monument to the sublime, and another to the ridiculous. The latter concerns two airmen who landed their vehicle on the mountain. The former (erected in 1890 by Canon Rawnsley and Miss Coombe) concerns Charles Gough, who in 1805 scaled the mountain with his dog. Stumbling near the summit, he fell, was killed, and lay there undiscovered. Three months later a shepherd noticed Gough's dog, emaciated but still on guard near his master. Wordsworth told the story, in a poem called 'Fidelity':

> The Dog had watched about the spot,
> Or by his master's side;
> How nourished there through such long time
> He knows, who gave that love sublime;
> And gave the strength of feeling, great
> Above all human estimate.

To remark that the dog had merely obeyed a bio-chemical instinct, does not lessen a sane man's wonder and admiration.

The views from Helvellyn reward a climber. The sea is there, the Scottish hills, and a large tract of the north country. Through glasses you can identify some of the villages and cottages. If you were sufficiently concerned you could discover how many of those cottages were owned by people who did not reside in Lakeland. You might even discover for how many—or how few—weeks they were occupied each year. Defoe remarked on the sturdiness of Lakeland domestic architecture: 'every gentleman's house is a castle'. He meant, of course, that all such houses had thick walls and that some adjoined a peel tower, as at Kentmere Hall, which stands alone in a steep valley near Staveley, a few miles from Windermere. As a guest at the Hall, I have seen its vaulted cellars and the dark stairway to the battlements. Kentmere Hall was the home of twelve generations of Gilpins, of whom the most famous—Bernard Gilpin—is still remembered as 'The Apostle of the North'. Born at Kentmere in 1517, Bernard Gilpin graduated at The Queen's College, Oxford, before continuing his studies at Paris and Louvain. In a sermon preached to King Edward VI he declared: 'A thousand pulpits in England are covered with dust, some have not had four sermons these fifteen or sixteen years, since friars left their limitations, and a few of those were worthie the name of sermons'. Practising his own preaching, Gilpin declined the bishopric of Carlisle, choosing rather to serve as parish priest in County Durham, whence he evangelised among the lawless dales of the Scottish border. In 1782 another member of the family, Rev William Gilpin, published a guidebook to Wales and the Wye Valley, followed by volumes about Westmorland, Cumberland, and the New Forest (the last being illustrated by his nephew, William Sawrey Gilpin, first president of the Royal Society of Painters in Water-Colours).

One wonders whether William Gilpin would have approved the Forestry Commission's vast acreage of conifer plantations. Wordsworth, as we know, disapproved: 'To those who plant for profit,' he wrote, 'I would utter first a regret that they should have selected these lovely vales for their vegetable manufactory'. Both Wordsworth and Gilpin would have mourned the death of so many elms, not only in Lakeland but also throughout England. The so-called Dutch Elm disease first appeared soon after World War I, carried by bark beetles. In its early stages the disease was relatively mild and generally localised, but during the 1970s it became a national epidemic, destroying millions of elms.

Wordsworth classified the Lakeland farmers as Estatesmen or owners of a small property which they cultivated for themselves. Such people, he added, were 'kindhearted, frank, and manly: prompt to serve without servility'. In many ways the Estatesmen were self-sufficient, as indeed they had to be, living in isolated valleys or on the slopes of bare mountains. An Estatesman's family produced most of its own food, turned its own wool and hide into garments and footwear, made its own entertainments, led its own life. It was they who inspired Wordsworth's 'plain living and high thinking', an ideal which the Romans described as *mens sana in corpore sano*.

The modern Estatesman is still in many ways a different breed from the holidaymakers who crowd his homeland. He feels proud of his calling. He agrees with the Edwardian farmhands whom Flora Thompson knew in Oxfordshire: 'It was a man's life, and they laughed scornfully at the occupation of some who looked down on them'. Young and old alike, the true Lakelanders retain an oldfashioned *tu* and *du* which, like the French and the Germans, they reserve for relatives and close friends. 'How eest thou?' is a common greeting. But if a stranger becomes too familiar he will find himself rebuked: 'Don't thee thou me. Thee thou them as thou's thee'. Such, then, were the men and women whom I met at cottages and farms as I travelled south to the region's smallest lake, Brothers Water, at the foot of Kirkstone Pass, so-named because some of its roadside rocks resemble a ruined kirk. On the summit of the Pass stands the only tavern ever to be founded by an Anglican priest. Its original purpose was to shelter travellers during rough weather, for in winter the Pass is often snowbound.

The road beyond Kirkstone delves deep, leaving Troutbeck on its right, high as a heavenly village. Thereafter I followed another and lonelier lane, halting at a point overlooking Windermere and the mountains beyond. Once more I sent greetings to old friends who, although they were out of sight, were ever in mind: Mrs Tyson of Watendlath (the Borrowdale home of Hugh Walpole's *Judith Paris*); the lane beside the western shore of Thirlmere; the roadless moorland between Shap Abbey and Haweswater; the fell ponies grazing near John Peel's Caldbeck; the secret byways (for such they are) within a few miles of Coniston Water; and Wordsworth's Dove Cottage at Grasmere, visited each year by hundreds of thousands of pilgrims who have never read his poetry (come to Dove Cottage in wintertime, when you will share Dorothy Wordsworth's benediction: 'It calls home the heart to quietness').

And so at last I reached Kendal, the southern Gateway to Lakeland. Although the local council has demolished many of the alleys that were the town's most endearing features, the ruined castle abides (birthplace of Henry VIII's fortunate widow, Katherine Parr), and in Wildman Street they have preserved the medieval Castle Dairy. George Romney, the artist, was married in Kendal. Having deserted his wife for thirty-seven years, he returned and soon afterwards died, nursed lovingly by the woman whom he had forsaken. Tennyson depicted the painter's delirium when he half-recognised his nurse:

Have I not met you somewhere long ago?
I am all but sure I have—in Kendal Church . . .

The last lap of my Westmorland journey ended at the little town of Kirkby Lonsdale, which I have long regarded as a second home. The town's name is Viking, the *by* or 'settlement' with a *kirk* or 'church' overlooking a dale of the River Lune. A plaque on a knoll near the church records Ruskin's opinion that the view therefrom is among the loveliest in England. Far below, the river weaves a labyrinth of blue loops among green pastures grazed by white sheep. High above, the fells rise up like dumb replicas of 'the great Huguenot psalm' which impressed Robert Bridges with its 'severe perfection of habitual grace'.

For more than twenty years I have watched while tourism nibbled at Kirkby Lonsdale, and in places bit deep. Many of the friendly shops have either ordered you to serve yourself or have become gift shops, tea shops, antique shops. The medieval bridge across the Lune has been marred by a car park and a hot dog stall. The meadows below the old school have become a housing estate, occupied chiefly by elderly strangers. Despite those assaults, Kirkby's inner fortress remains intact. Progress has not yet 'developed' Jingling Lane, Tram Lane, Horsemarket, Fairbank, and the forge where Jonty Wilson still plies an ancient craft. Kirkby Lonsdale in winter recovers its true identity as the home of ordinary men and women who, on acquaintance, reveal how extraordinary everyone is. Stand fast, little town, against the Philistines!

So, I passed through Lakeland, the highest and most majestic corner of England, a region given over to tourism, yet studded with pockets of resistance whose natives blend the best of the old and the new. Concrete yards, for example, have replaced mudbound cattle mires. Women no longer draw water from a well. Electricity brings instant warmth and light. Ambulance, fire brigade, school bus, mobile library, mobile grocery, district nurse . . . all those boons now serve farms and cottages which formerly could be reached only after a slow journey along rough tracks. When winter brings its annual respite, a modern Estatesman shares Wordsworth's gratitude for being surrounded

> Not with the mean and vulgar works of man,
> But with high objects, with enduring things—
> With life and nature . . .

8 THE MARCHES

The Marches or Welsh border counties stretch from the northern to the southern half of England; more precisely, from Cheshire to Gloucestershire. The variety within that region precludes a succinct description of the whole, for the Marches are an amalgam of several regions. Thus, Cheshire is a northern county; Shropshire and Herefordshire are in the Midlands;

Bleatarn House, near Little Langdale, Cumbria
Wordsworth said that the Lakeland cottages and farmhouses seem 'to have arisen, by an instinct of their own, out of the native rock — so little is there in them of formality, such is their wildness and beauty'. Built of local stone, the old Lakeland homes are indeed as indigenous as mushrooms. This farmhouse stands under the shadow of the Langdale Pikes in what used to be Westmorland. Wordsworth knew many such places:

> a small hereditary farm . . .
> Remote from view of city spire, or sound
> Of minster clock . . .

Although the Pikes are not the highest in Lakeland, they reveal an impressive silhouette. Oats and root crops are grown on the foothills, but, as in Ribblesdale, the staple commodity is sheep, chiefly the Herdwicks that can thrive in conditions which would kill many a lowland breed.

Gloucestershire adjoins the Westcountry. The prevalence of red sandstone throughout the Marches might cause a traveller to fancy himself in the Quantocks. On the heights of Clun Forest in Shropshire the same traveller might fancy himself among the Northumbrian Cheviots, though the Clun contours are gentler and milder. It is as though Nature had consciously inserted a nether region between the Saxon Midlands and the Welsh Highlands. G. M. Trevelyan, a sceptical man, admitted that the Marches are numinous: 'Places where the fairies dwell lie for the part west of the Avon'. Mary Webb, a Marcher poet, said the same thing in verse:

A lone green valley, good for sheep,
Where still the ancient fairies keep
Their right of way and copyhold . . .

Chipping Camden, Gloucestershire

Built centuries ago by local craftsmen using local stone, the Cotswold churches and houses confirm the poet's vision:

Mellow in moonlight, warm by day,
The Cotswold hamlets stood
Like hospices along the way
To beauty's brotherhood.

Chipping Camden — sometimes called 'The Queen of the Cotswolds' — is an ancient market town, whence its Old English name, *ciepping* or 'market' in a *campadenu* or 'fortified valley'. Baptist Hicks, first Viscount Camden, was buried in the stately church. The present viscounty is a courtesy title borne by the Earls of Gainsborough since 1841. Chipping Camden had its own seventeenth-century Wonder, William Harrison, who suddenly vanished and was presumed to have been murdered. Some years later he returned home and learned that his two 'murderers' had been hanged. John Masefield wrote a play about it, called *A Camden Wonder*. In 1929 the Camden Trust was formed to defend the town against 'development'.

The Marches take their name from the Germanic *mark* which originally meant 'waste land', but came to mean any boundary between nations and tribes. England undoubtedly faced a threat from the Welsh tribes, which is why William the Conqueror encouraged certain of his vassals to seize estates on both sides of the border and then to govern them with a minimum of royal intervention. These Marcher Lordships included the counties of Denbigh, Montgomery, Radnor, Brecon, and Monmouth, together with much of west Shropshire and west Herefordshire, as well as small areas of Pembrokeshire, Carmarthenshire, Cardiganshire, Merionethshire, Worcestershire, and Gloucestershire. To ensure that no Marcher Lord became over-powerful, William sent four of his most trusted friends to supervise the region from castles at Chester, Shrewsbury, Hereford, and Montgomery.

The subjugation of Wales was inevitable because the Welsh threatened the peace and security of England. Nevertheless, the Marcher Lords allowed their Welsh subjects to retain Welsh law, and their English subjects to retain English law. If a case involved both Welsh and English litigants, it was tried by a body of Anglo-Welsh law, known as the Custom of the Lordship. The Lords governed the Marches until Edward IV established the Court of the President and Council of Wales and the Marches. Henry VII, himself a Welshman, used that Court in order to impose further restrictions on the Marcher Lords; and in 1535 Henry VIII not only declared the Marches to be 'incorporated, united and annexed to and with the Realm of England', but also compelled the Welsh nobility and gentry to become anglicised: 'no person or persons that use the Welsh speech or language shall have . . . any office . . . within the realm of England, Wales, or other the King's Dominion . . . unless he or they use and exercise the King's speech or language'. Not every Welshman resented the annexation. Lord Herbert of Cherbury's *Life and Reign of King Henry VIII* quoted a Welsh petition to the King: 'We . . . inhabiting that part of the island which our invaders first called Wales . . . do crave to be receiv'd and adopted into the same laws and privileges which your other subjects enjoy'. Between 1536 and 1542 the union of the two nations was confirmed in three Statutes whereby Wales retained its own

144

assizes or Courts of the King's Great Session; Monmouthshire alone being rated as a quasi-English county. The Council of Wales and the Welsh Marches survived as an administrator and judiciary for personal pleas until, in 1689, the government of the Principality was divided between the Lords Lieutenants of North Wales and South Wales. When the Great Sessions were abolished in 1830, the administrative and political systems of the two nations became identical. The Marcher Lords, however, did not utterly perish, for the Mayor of Newport in Pembrokeshire remains *ex officio* Lord Marcher of the Barony of Kemaes, which Henry VIII excluded from his abolition of the Marcherships.

The English conquest of Wales fulfilled the policy of the Romans, who had built roads and forts in many parts of the Principality, with Chester as a northernmost *castra* or 'military base'. Cheshire was originally *Castra legionum* or 'Camp of the legions'. In 1232 the Earldom of Chester was held by John, Earl of Huntingdon, nephew of the Scottish King. When John died without issue, the earldom was purchased by the English King as a defence against the Welsh. By long custom the Prince of Wales is *de jure* Earl of Chester. These royal associations are emphasised by the marching song of the Cheshire Regiment, an ancient Scottish air—'Wha wouldna'a fecht for Charlie?'—recalling the loyalty of the Cheshire farmers who sheltered Charles II at Boscobel.

Chester preserves enough old houses to suggest what the medieval city looked like. Indeed, Britain has nothing to excel the timbered architecture in Eastgate Street, Bridge Street and Watergate Street, where the overhanging storeys of two-tiered shops create a covered promenade. The city walls, extending for nearly two miles, were built by the Romans and then enlarged in 907 by Ethelfleda, Lady of the Mercians. Occupying the site of a Saxon church, the cathedral was an abbey from the twelfth to the sixteenth century. Its Norman pillars recall the dour strength of Durham Cathedral. Chester, in short, is an illustrated history of England from Roman to Atomic times.

Although the Marches between Chester and Shrewsbury offer impressive vistas, the main roads carry such a heavy burden of commercial traffic that travellers no longer share Coleridge's ambition 'to write a Sonnet to the Road between Wem and

Shrewsbury, and immortalise every step of it'. I, too, have walked every step of it, and was all the while reminded of my mortality, so fast and furious were the vehicles.

At Shrewsbury the gateway to Roger de Montgomery's castle survives, as also do Ireland's mansion and Owen's mansion, the timbered homes of Tudor merchants; but the town is dominated by industry, and has therefore ceased to deserve Mary Webb's allegiance:

> A fair town is Shrewsbury—
> The world over
> You'll hardly find a fairer,
> In its fields of clover . . .

As Wordsworth speaks for Lakeland, so Mary Webb speaks for the Marches. Some years ago I made a pilgrimage to her various Shropshire homes: Stanton-upon-Hine-Heath, where she lived as a child; Meole Brace, now a suburb of Shrewsbury, where she lived as a young woman; Church Stretton, where she spent her honeymoon; Pontesbury, where, in a house called Roseville, she wrote *The Golden Arrow*; and Lyth Hill, where she and her husband built a house and then set up as market gardeners, selling their produce in Shrewsbury. Like Emily Brontë, Mary Webb spent almost the whole of her life in her native region. She died relatively young, and was remembered—if at all—as an author whose work had failed to attract much notice. Although she never complained, a hint of heartache crept into *Precious Bane*, where a character cries: 'I was like one standing at the lane end with a nosegay to offer to the world as it rode by. But the world rode me down . . rode me down'.

Soon after Mary Webb's death, the prime minister, Stanley Baldwin, made a speech at the Royal Literary Fund dinner, in which, as a man of the Marches, he praised her work, saying that its strength 'lies in the fusion of the elements of nature and man, as observed in this remote countryside'. Baldwin's speech made Mary Webb famous overnight. Her publishers could scarcely meet the demand for books that had hitherto lain unsold. *Precious Bane* was re-printed twelve times in twelve months; the poems and essays were re-printed twenty-three times in twenty years.

Posterity has accepted Baldwin's verdict: 'The stupid urban view of country life as dull receives a fresh and crushing answer in the books of Mary Webb'. Despite her mysticism—or perhaps because of it—Mary Webb plumbed the abyss of human motive. Her poetry and prose are maps of the Marcher Country as it was until the 1920s. With a tilt at Housman, G. K. Chesterton once remarked: 'Much of the noble, though more neglected work of Mary Webb might be called the prose poems of a Shropshire Lass'. Her books were indeed a labour of love: 'Shropshire,' she declared, 'is a county where the dignity and beauty of ancient things lingers long, and I have been fortunate . . . in being born and brought up in the magical atmosphere'.

South of Shrewsbury I once had an adventure. It occurred in 1955 while I was walking from John o'Groats to Land's End via Wales and as many byways as could be compressed into twenty miles a day for ten weeks. Somewhere between Shrewsbury and Church Stretton I suddenly rebelled against the traffic. Refusing any longer to be jostled and fume-fouled, I climbed a gate, crossed a couple of meadows, and there sat down, wondering how to reach Presteigne in peace. Consulting the map, I noticed a track, marked as *Roman Road*, leading toward my destination. The track was Watling Street; not *the* Watling Street from Dover to Wroxeter, but one of several minor roads that came to be called Watling Street. So, while the traffic roared along the highway, I walked quietly along a byway with primrosed grass down the middle, and a bevy of blackbirds above, each singing the same song in a different way. On my right the Long Mynd stretched like a green spine; on my left, a wood gleamed with bluebells. After several miles the old road was joined by the modern one, but not for long, because at Craven Arms the Roman road went its own way as a lane at the foot of wooded hills. On my latest revisitation I ought to have followed that lane, and indeed I would have followed it, had not the silence echoed visually from a signpost pointing to Clun.

Clunton and Clunbury,
Clungerford and Clun,
Are the quietest places
Under the sun.

Was Clun still as quiet as in Housman's Edwardian heydays? In order to find out, I went there, along eight miles of what used to be the main London road, known locally as Long Lane.

Clun *was* quiet. In fact, it was so quiet that my footsteps echoed through the miniature market square. But no one appeared.

As to size, Clun is a village, set on a knoll above the River Clun. Many of its houses are old, timbered, whitewashed. At one time the parish was the largest in England, covering more than a hundred and fifty square miles, chiefly of forest. As to status, Clun is a town, with a charter from Edward II. The Almshouse contains the ceremonial sword which symbolised the jurisdiction of the manorial court of the Lord Marcher of Clun.

And still no one appeared.

Clun Almshouse was founded as the Holy Trinity Hospital by the Earl of Northampton during the reign of James I. Passing through an iron gate, you see a lawn and a row of comely stone cottages, pierced by an ancient timber door; and beyond the timber door you see another lawn, flanked by other cottages. The Hospital now accommodates twelve old men, each having his own bedroom and sitting room. Prayers are said twice daily in the chapel, but the almsfolk no longer wear their distinctive uniform, nor do they dine together in hall.

And still no one appeared.

I strolled across to a grocer's shop, and glanced through the open door. If I had dropped a pin, the echo might have aroused the proprietor. But I had no pin, and was reluctant to raise my voice lest it boomed like thunder through the June sunlight. Still treading softly, for fear of breaking the spell, I went down to the river and a medieval bridge whence I glanced up at the ruins of a hilltop castle; and after that I deliberately played truant by revisiting Offa's Dyke, three miles north of Clun, built during the eighth century by King Offa of Mercia, partly as a frontier and partly as a road that would carry troops to any sector where danger threatened. The Dyke extends from Prestatyn in North Wales to a field on the Gloucestershire bank of the Wye near Chepstow. Today it is a public footpath, in some places almost worn away by tillage and time; in other places a wide green track, flanked by a ditch. I followed the Dyke across some fields and then over a stream beside a black-and-white farmhouse. There the green mound became higher, climbing and dipping through a bloodstained border region which, like its Scottish equivalent, now lay at peace. If you seek the English Marches *in excelsis*, follow Offa's Dyke to Middle Knuck and Church Town, switchbacking over the crest of hills and into the depths of valleys. So far as I recollect, you pass only three houses on your way; and at Church Town you find only two (one of them a ruin). Forgetful of Watling Street, I followed that switchback, on and on and on, accompanied by blossom and birdsong and sunlight. I might easily have ended at Snowdon, or in Flintshire, or among the Wirral marshes. *Sed Deus flavit*. At about six o'clock the sky darkened, the breeze dropped, the storm broke, and I ran for shelter.

'Well,' said the farmer's wife, 'we don't really take visitors unless we know them. But ...' she stepped back from the rain, 'you'd better come inside.'

The rafters of the living room were blacker than ebony; the hearth was fragrant with cherry wood. Two boiled eggs arrived, both brown; honey from the bees, bread from the oven, ham from the piggery. There followed three hours of fireside talk with people who, if they governed England, would soon bring most of us to our senses, and the rest to an emigration office. At ten o'clock the staircase creaked, the bath boiled, the mattress feathered, the rain ceased, the owl hooted, the silence sang, and the truant slept.

Next morning broke so warm that we egg-and-baconed with the kitchen windows wide open, serenaded by cuckoos and one robin astride a pile of logs in the yard.

At noon I was back on the lane which I ought never to have left. Sometimes it deviated from the course of Watling Street. At other times the Street itself deviated from a straight line, as at Berryhill, where it turned south-west. When at last the Street disappeared in a field, I joined a lane that led to the Street's destination, Leintwardine or *Bravinium*, formerly a small Roman settlement, now a pleasant village at the confluence of two tributaries of the River Severn. Pleasant, too, was the weather, our much – maligned climate, whose course between the extremes of heat and cold is best appreciated by Englishmen who have sailed the Red Sea or dwelt in Siberia.

The lane from Leintwardine to Lingen was just as narrow as I remembered it, just as peaceful, just as sheep-speckled. Lingen itself was still a hamlet sans inn or shop; still so silent that the lambs sounded loud. In the churchyard stands a 1914-18 memorial to the Englishmen who died in order that we might live and likewise defend our liberty. In 1955, while I was counting the four names on that memorial, the church clock struck four, announcing a coincidence which still chimes through the decades of memory. A second recollection of 1955 concerned a Leintwardine man who had told me that the old coach road led from Lingen to Presteigne. I did not then trouble to reply that no coach had ever crossed the dizzy hills separating those two places. However, I did resolve to seek Lingen's opinion of the legend. The search proved difficult, for I arrived at teatime, when the sun was so hot that even the youngest dog lay flat-out among whatever shade it could find. Noticing an open door, I knocked. The echo merged with the tick of a grandfather clock and one wasp walking wearily on the window. Flowers I could smell, and a whiff of floor polish; but nobody answered. It was Clun all over again. I then tried at a farmhouse; and there also, through open windows, I smelt flowers, and heard a wasp and a clock and nothing else until a cuckoo called. At the third house—a cottage with honeysuckle on the wall—an old woman slept in an old chair in an old porch. I therefore passed by, not wishing to disturb her. 'Anyway,' I murmured, glancing at the hills, 'even the Valkyrie would think twice before driving a coach-and-four over that skyline.' Ten seconds later I was contradicted by a farmhand who appeared from behind a hedge.

'You canna' mistake the way,' he said. 'Just follow your nose.'
'And that really was the coach road? I can't believe it.'
'My grandfather believed it.'
'Why?'
'Because he was the coachman.'
'Up those hills?'
'And down again.'
'But . . .'
'But not with the passengers on board. Everyone had to get

out and heave. And if any o' the women wouldn't budge, my grandfather used to shout: "All ladies under forty please to get out." That shifted 'em.'

What a fickle creature memory is; sometimes honest, sometimes deceitful. Retravelling the old coach road, I was able to anticipate every bend and every gradient, even the one that dropped like a precipice. Alas, they had removed the old signboard: *Steep Hill, Cyclists Are Advised To Dismount.*

On, then, I went, down and up and up, delving among woods and beside meadows nearly ripe for reaping; to the tune of so many birds that their song seemed to be a baton which they passed down the line of the sky. On the summit, I knew what to expect. Gazing south, I saw England, spread like flattened map. The fields were patched with sandstone furrows. White farms winked golden windows. Brooks burned blue. Blossom waved a flag of truce. And over all stood Hay Bluff, that inland cliff, jutting like the paw of a gigantic lion. Having saluted my own land, I turned to greet Wales, which was less varied than England, but not less steep, for there also the hills rose up, and beyond them the mountains that multiplied until they reached their sum at Snowdon.

The last three miles of England were easy going because the lane loped downhill, passing a house, a cottage, and then two more cottages. On reaching level ground, I sighted the roofs of Presteigne and a bridge across the River Lugg, dividing England from Wales. On each side of the bridge several white ducks preened and plunged and went contentedly about their lawful occasions. Beyond the bridge, the Welsh street was flanked by old and therefore handsome houses. For old times' sake I played truant again, on this occasion by crossing the river into another land. Somebody—I forget who—said that the nations of the world ought to preserve their own identity and to foster universal amity. The nations themselves, however, have chosen to dilute their identity and to whittle away their amity. Thus it is that certain far-flung peoples buy American cars, eat French food, collect Japanese cameras, speak pidgeon English, and spend much time killing one another. Even among the wiley Welsh there are some who would like to recruit their own army, to manufacture their own bows and arrows, to banish the alien residents who help to subsidise Wales, and to attract tourists by plastering the countryside with tongue-twisting monoglot signposts. Happily, I have never yet encountered any of those fanatics at Presteigne. Always I have been received courteously by a warmhearted and businesslike people who know very well that much of their bread is buttered on the English side.

Despite an outbreak of industry along its outskirts, Presteigne is an exception to the rule that few Welsh towns are beautiful. An abundance of local timber allowed these Marcher counties to achieve something less dour than the grey and slate-roofed buildings of northern and central Wales. Formerly the smallest of all the Welsh capitals, Presteigne may justly repeat William Saxton's opinion: 'Prestayn for beauteous building is the best in the Shire'. The shops in the narrow high street combine old-fashioned courtesy with up-to-date conversation: 'Lewis is playing scrum-half again, I see. A marvel, that boy. He gets the ball out to the wing before the referee can blow his whistle. And religious, too, mark you. They say he can sink ten pints and still recite the Lord's Prayer. A credit to Wales is Lewis Jones.'

After Presteigne I took B4355, that being the lifeless label slapped by motorists on a Marcher road meandering along the border within sight of Radnor Forest. Somewhere near Titley I re-entered Herefordshire, the county whose capital was built beside a ford on a *Hereath* or 'military road'. The two great houses at Titley are the Court (a seventeenth-century mansion) and Eywood (seat of the eighteenth-century Earls of Oxford). From Lingen south to Cusop the Herefordshire border is an unspoiled panorama of hills and valleys and woods. Some of the houses are red sandstone; others present a half-timbered magpie façade. This was the land of John Masefield, Poet Laureate of England, who praised it in prose: 'For some years, like many children, I lived in Paradise, or, rather, like a specially lucky child in two Paradises linked together by a country of exceeding beauty and strangeness . . . The linked Paradises are parted from each other by some hilly miles of rural England and by two of the English rivers'.

Still surrounded by hills, I reached Kington, a *cyne-tun* or 'King's manor' belonging to Edward the Confessor. Kington is a steep little town beside the River Arrow, much troubled by traffic through the narrow street. A modernised Grammar School retains some features of the original building, founded by the widow of Sir John Hawkins, a Tudor seaman. Lady Hawkins was a member of the Vaughan family at Hergest Court, now a farmhouse. Kington begat a histrionic celebrity, Stephen Kemble (brother of Sarah Siddons), who was born in the town and very nearly on the stage, since the happy event occurred a few minutes after the final curtain of Shakespeare's *King Henry the Eighth*, in which Mrs Kemble, wife of the impressario, was playing Anne Bullen. Sarah Siddons had been born in comparable circumstances and not a great way off, at Brecon, where her father's Company of Comedians were performing. Stephen Kemble became a chemist's assistant, but soon followed his father's footsteps and ultimately outpaced them, for he played Othello at Covent Garden, and was buried in Durham Cathedral.

James Guthrie's memoir of Edward Thomas contains a warning: 'It is almost a shame to be so explicit about any quiet spot, for fear of the motorist, whose search for peace is the beginning of destruction'. Concerning my journey from Kington to Hay-on-Wye I shall say only that it twisted and switchbacked through a solitude more beautiful than any other sector of my travels. The perfect June weather confirmed an opinion which I had reached long ago, that the best parts of The Marches contain the most delectable scenery in England. The same view was held by a Scottish poet, Andrew Young, who described the district as 'so sweet and yet so impressive that it might be considered the most beautiful part of England . . .'. By following zany lanes and by halting at many hilltops I was able to spend three hours on a journey which the main roads could have spanned in thirty minutes. Time after time I stopped at a gap in the hedge, or beside a gate in the bank, and there turned my head slowly, so that England passed into Wales, and Wales re-entered England, as though on a revolving stage. Thus occupied, I eventually reached Hay-on-Wye, the Norman *La Haie* or 'The enclosed place', called by the Welsh *Trelli* or 'town in the forest'.

Hay stands in Breconshire, but keeps one toe in Herefordshire, which is where they seat the railway station. Hay is a high and bustling little town. Its streets are either narrow or not quite so narrow. Its market square is a meeting place of two ancient enemies who long ago signed a truce, but without pledging themselves to an effusive affection. On market day the conversation encompasses country life: 'Shocking, the price of beef last week. How do they expect a farmer to pay his overdraft?' . . . 'Evan Morgan's eldest wanted the latest fashion, so she cycled all the way to Hereford' . . . 'In Merfyn's parish the vicar preaches real lovely. And so short, too. That's what I like. Six minutes only and he's made his point, and we go straight into "And now to God the Father".'

The best guide to these parts is an Englishman, Rev Francis Kilvert, who from 1865 until 1872 served as curate of Clyro, just beyond Hay. His diary is a classic of local landscapes, legends, customs, scandals, and characters at a time when the Anglo-Welsh border was more self-conscious than it is now. For example, Kilvert mentions a house that stood half in England and half in Wales: 'Old Betty Williams of Crowther used to tell me about the birth of a child in this house (the Pant) and the care taken that the child should be born in England in the English corner of the cottage. "Stand there, Betsy, in this corner," said the midwife. And the girl was delivered of the child *standing.*' Much addicted to adjectives, Kilvert strung six of them into a necklace that fits the Celtic temperament: 'impulsive, warm-hearted, excitable, demonstrative, imaginative, eloquent' (he ought to have added 'melancholy'). When the sun began to set, I saw Hay as Kilvert saw it: 'A lovely evening and the Black Mountains lighted up grandly, all the furrows and water courses clear and brilliant. People coming home from market, birds singing, buds bursting, and the spring air full of beauty, life and hope'.

At Hay-on-Wye, as in the Scottish Border Country, three routes beckoned me, but on this occasion only one of them could be followed. Should I take the mountain road to Capel-y-ffyn and Landor's old home beside the ruins of Llanthony Abbey? Should I go via Cusop (three of its churchyard yews are older than Domesday), where Dallas Brook divides England from Wales? Or should I enter the Golden Valley? I chose the Valley, chiefly because I had never seen it. Having seen, I understood

154

why some people accept its name as an example of poetic justice, though the original form—from the Welsh *ystrad*—meant simply 'a valley'. Domesday Book Latinised *ystrad* into *stradelia* and then prefixed a tautological *vallis* to produce *Vallis Stradelia*. The Normans, however, discovered that the region was watered by the river Our, which they mistranslated as *Or*, meaning 'gold'. So, the valley became 'Golden' while the river became *D'Or* and ultimately 'Dore'.

The Valley's northern approach lies near Dorstone, named after a cromlech, Arthur's Stone, overlooking eleven counties. At this point the Valley is wide and rather shallow. Near Peterchurch—where the hills grow taller—stands three ancient buildings: Wellbrook Manor, a fourteenth-century house with a raftered hall; Snodhill Court, a Jacobean house with gabled dormers and a nail-gnarled door; and the ruins of Snodhill Castle, once the property of King Stephen. Midway along the Valley lies Vowchurch, drowsing among Tudor cottages and a bridge across the Dore. In 1291 the place was called *Powchirche*, the 'many-coloured church'. Why, I do not know. Perhaps the Norman church contained some especially vivid murals, long since faded or plastered over. The scene outside the church was certainly many-coloured. Westward the Black Mountains evoked Masefield's memories: 'I learned at a very early age something of the feeling of the border, where the two races met but did much mingle'. Nor were those suspicions confined to veterans: 'The feeling was shared by young and old . . .'.

Since leaving Hay I had met only three cars, and in the Valley itself I had met no vehicle at all, nor anyone nearer than a distant herdsman quizzing his red-and-white Herefords. Forgetful that fields and meadows cannot be incessantly ploughed and reaped, a townsman half-believes that the land farms itself without human intervention. At other times, when entering a silent hamlet, he suspects that the houses, too, maintain themselves unaided. I came very near to sharing those illusions when I reached Bacton, which lay in a backwater off the lane, as though to justify the name of one of its cottages, Paradise. The great house, New Court, had been rebuilt since the days of its most illustrious occupant, Blanche Parry, chief gentlewoman of Queen Elizabeth's Privy Council. The church altar cloth is thought to have been made by Blanche herself who, like her royal mistress, never married. 'With maiden queen,' said her monument, 'a maid did end her life.' Blanche Parry went blind in her old age, and died when she was eighty-two, deeply mourned by the Queen who had known her since childhood.

Beyond Bacton the Valley grew narrower and steeper. The lane twisted like an uphill horse. The houses, which never had been numerous, disappeared. Everything slept, or seemed to sleep. Even the cattle stood still, drenched in sunlight. Suddenly, on my left, only a few yards from the lane, a tower loomed above firs and apple trees; and there stood Abbey Dore, alone among fields. The monastery was founded for Cistercians in 1147 by Robert FitzHarold, grandson of the Earl of Hereford. Its lonely situation suited the monks, the foremost sheep breeders in Christendom. Of that abbey nothing remains. Most of the present church was built c1180. Soon after its dissolution in 1535 the church began to decay, and was bought by John Scudamore, whose great-great-grandson, 'the good Lord Scudamore', repaired the fabric in 1632. John Aubrey witnessed the desecration of some of the statues: 'A little before I saw them,' he wrote, 'a mower had taken off one of the armes to whett his syth'. Viscount Scudamore paid for the roof to be rebuilt in oak by John Abel, nicknamed 'The King's Architect' because he designed defences for the Royalists when they were beseiged at Shrewsbury. The oak cost five shillings per ton. Re-consecration took place on Palm Sunday 1634, the anniversary of the viscount's birthday. Seen from outside, Abbey Dore resembles a large parish church; seen from within, it resembles a small cathedral, being lofty, well lit by many windows, and embellished with Abel's oak roof and furniture. The only monastic relic is a blocked doorway in the north wall, whence a staircase led to the dormitory.

As at Lingen and Clun, no one appeared in the Golden Valley; yet this was noon on a warm June day. Perhaps all the people were indoors, listening to news of the latest bomb, strike, demonstration, by-election, and any other event which impedes mankind in the difficult task of trying to extract brief enjoyment from a long journey through a vale of tears. Myself, I rested in a meadow, listening to the birds while sunlight sparkled on the hawthorn blossom. *Cantate Domino*, cried the Psalmist: 'O sing unto the Lord a new song . . .'. As I went my way I did sing a song albeit in prose and ex tempore while I walked: O the beauty of an English summer day, when the sun shines high and hot from a cloudless sky, and a breeze tempers the sting, and every meadow and all the hills wear a new-laundered livery of green, and the livery is trimmed with white blossom and yellow buttercups and the bluebells that chime silently like the wavelets of a painted ocean. O the daylong arc of scent and sight and sound, rising ecstatically from dawn's dim chorus, climbing leisurely to fervid noon, slanting serenely to the last late thrush and a rose-pink aura in the west. There are not many such days; twenty perhaps—sometimes thirty—in one year; yet when they come and while they last, all save the heaviest heart leaps up to greet them; and even heaviness may lean on them, sharing its burden.

My own burden—a small haversack—provided refreshments at Ewyas Harold, the home of the abbey's founder; and at about one o'clock, after some agreeable detours, I crossed the border into Monmouthshire, an anglicised county, studded with Welsh place-names: Llanvihangel-Ystern-Llewern, Mynydd Llan-wenarth, Llantilio-Crossenny, Llanvaches, Llangwm-Isaf, Pen-y-Clawdd, Llanddewi-Rhydderch, and (as an instance of bi-lingualism) Llangattock-nigh-Usk. An Englishman abroad in the Marches may be helped to understand—though scarcely to pronounce—some of the common Welsh words, as follows: *aber* (estuary), *afon* (river), *betws* (chapel), *caer* (fort), *cwm* (valley), *llan* (church), *llyn* (lake), *nant* (brook), *pen* (headland), *porth* (harbour), *tre* (village). The spate of l, y, and w in the Welsh language makes up for the absence of j, k, q, v, x, z.

When Rev Evans surveyed Monmouthshire in 1809 he found many villages where 'divine service is performed wholly in Welsh . . .'. The natives, he added, 'retain their ancient prejudice, and still brand everything assimilating to English with the opprobrious epithet of Saxon'. Sixty years later, George Borrow said what needed to be said: 'Monmouthshire is at present considered an English county, though certainly with little reason, for it not only stands on the western side of the Wye, but the names of almost all its parishes are Welsh, and many thousands of its population still speak the Welsh language'. During the 1960s the county contained about ten thousand Welsh-speakers, of whom a few spoke no English at all.

The Golden Valley ended near Grosmont (*Grosso Monte* or 'Big Hill'), the county's third largest town until it was ravaged by fire, and thereafter became a village with a steep street, a Regency market hall, and a church that was built for Eleanor of Provence, Queen to Henry III. Among the local houses are Lower Dyffryn, once a seat of the Welsh Sitsyllts, who, having Englished themselves as Cecil, rose to power under Queen Elizabeth I, and are still eminent in scholarship and politics. The pinnacle of Grosmont is a thirteenth-century moated castle, a gift from King John to Hubert de Burgh. In 1232 the Welsh attacked it at night; in 1405 they captured it by day; whereafter peace reigned, and the castled decayed. My own favourite corner

Luccumbe, Somerset

'The poor cottager contenteth himself with Cob for his Walls'. So wrote Richard Carew, the Westcountry poet. Cob, in fact, was called 'the poor man's masonry'. It seems to have been introduced by Crusaders who had admired the cob-walled palaces of Islam. The simplest cob is a mix of mud and chippings, bound together with straw and farmyard dung. A stronger mix contains sand and loam and clay. Cob being highly porous, an old maxim asserted that cob cottages need 'a wide hat and stout shoes' . . . that is, thatched eaves and rubble foundations. Periodically scraped and refilled, a cob house will stand for centuries.

These cob cottages lie between the Severn Sea and the edge of Exmoor. The Perpendicular parish church has one of the towers for which Somerset is famous. In 1612 Dr Henry Byam succeeded his father as rector of Luccumbe. Evicted by the Roundheads, he followed the King into hazardous exile, and was ultimately appointed a canon of Exeter and a prebendary of Wells. He died in his ninetieth year, and was buried in Luccumbe church.

of Grosmont lies beside the river, where a whitewashed farmhouse overlooks a small bridge under an arc of hills.

At Grosmont I was in familiar territory again, and therefore knew that the Marches did not dwindle to an anti-climax, but went their steep way unspoiled until they dipped to the River Severn, and foundered in an industrial Sargasso. Time had dealt gently with this corner of England. At Skenfrith the cottages looked the same as they had looked forty years ago. The lane looked the same, and so did the church. Beside its bridge across the River Monmow, the old mill still mused. Trees still clustered on the heights above the castle, one of the Trilateral Castles—the others being Grosmont and White—given by King John to de Burgh, his faithful Justiciar.

Somewhere between Skenfrith and Maypole a farmer was quizzing his hayfield. I halted, hoping to pass a pleasant time of

Near Burford, Oxfordshire

'Wherever I look or travel in England,' wrote John Ruskin, 'I see that men, wherever they can reach, destroy all beauty. Every perfect and lovely spot which they can touch, they defile.' It is a sign of the times that the Council for the Preservation of Rural England has lately re-named itself the Council for the *Protection* of Rural England.

Some people believe that these gawky pylons are beautiful. Some believe that they actually improve the look of the land. Others, by contrast, wish that the neccessary excrescences could be buried underground. Their inescapable presence seems especially painful in the Cotswolds, where almost every building, from the largest abbey to the humblest barn, is of local stone, like the wall which flanks the pylons.

Parts of the wall may be a century old, perhaps two centuries. Skill, sweat, and patience went to the making of that wall, every yard of it being designed to achieve a proper tension and a lasting equilibrium.

day; but the interlude proved unpleasant because a car drove by, containing two black men. Seeing them, the farmer scowled. 'British subjects, eh? If they lived here for a thousand years they still wouldn't be British.'

What does one say to that sort of remark? Or, rather, what does an Englishman say, trying to be fair to the world in general and to his fellowcountrymen in particular? Some people are unable to understand that the colour of one's skin does not itself create a bar. The bar is built of centuries of different ideals, different languages, different customs and cultures and religions and—no less important—different genes, those undemocratic entities, which are not members of the Disunited Nations.

'My daughter,' the farmer was saying, 'can't get a house to live in. And her husband's been out of work since January. Yet we still flood the country with foreigners. And another thing, Mister. What's the point of electing a government if half the electorate refuse to obey it? We might just as well hand over to the shop stewards. At least it'd save the cost of a general election.'

'But . . .'

'But I'm no Tory, mind. And I'm not a Socialist either. I'm not anything. The whole bunch of 'em aren't worth voting for. The Tories are pink, the Socialists are Reds, and if the Liberals lose any more seats they won't be a party at all . . . They'll be a bloody tête-à-tête. If I were twenty years younger I'd pack up and go to a real country. New Zealand or somewhere.' He pointed a finger at me. 'Did *you* think you'd live to see the day when an Englishman is sent to prison simply for saying he wants to sell his house to an Englishman?'

'Maybe . . .'

'Maybe he did go about it the wrong way. But two wrongs don't make a right.'

Now the farmer himself was at heart a kindly man and reasonably well-informed, as the rest of our conversation proved. Had a coloured family knocked at his door in distress, he would have offered them shelter and fellowship; and I fancy he would have enjoyed hearing about their un-English way of life in Africa or in India. But he never would enjoy witnessing the slow infiltration by aliens (people, that is, from another nation), nor would he ever understand those of his fellowcountrymen who not only encouraged it but also forbade him to speak his mind freely.

'The damage is done,' he said. And again he pointed his finger at me. 'You mark my words, Mister. One of these days there's going to be trouble. Real trouble. England's had it . . . the England that you and me knew. It's kaput. No bloody good.'

Right or wrong, the man meant what he said, and his words darkened my journey into Monmouth. Fortunately, however, there is a limit to our duty—and, indeed, to our ability—to brood on evils which we did not cause and are powerless to avert. After a few miles, therefore, I forgot the future, and was able once again to admire the present prospect of rolling hills and white farmhouses and young summer.

Few towns possess an entrance so stately as Monmouth's thirteenth-century bridge. The gatehouse above the single arch was manned throughout the Middle Ages, the Civil War, and the Chartist Riots. From that bridge the medieval citizens levied a toll on every ship carrying goods for sale within the town. The road beyond the bridge climbs to Agincourt Square and a statue of Monmouth's most famous native, King Henry V, who assured Captain Fluellen: 'I am Welsh, too, good countryman'. Monmouth Grammar School was founded in 1614 by a Gloucestershire draper who would have been appalled by the envy which has destroyed the English grammar schools, replacing them with academies designed not to offend the dunces. A third local celebrity was the Hon Charles Stewart Rolls, partner to Frederick Royce, a motor manufacturer.

Thomas Gray said of Monmouth: 'It lies in a vale that is the delight of my eyes . . .'. From the vale a lane climbs to Trelleck, a village with two inns, a hairpin bend, and traces of a Roman road which emphasised once again the Roman legacy, for less than a mile away stood one of thousands of parish churches; less than five miles away stood an abbey; and all had come via Rome. Equally perdurable was the Roman language, Latin, which for nearly two thousand years served as the Esperanto of educated Christendom.

Until the middle of the twentieth century, Latin formed part of an English liberal education. It is still used by every doctor, lawyer, botanist, chemist, and (in a debased form) by every scientist. Latin ranks next after Greek among the literatures of the ancient world. Our own literature was nurtured on Latin and thereafter on the Authorised Version of the Bible. Latin and Greek are two kinds of music, each sharpening an Englishman's ear for the melody of his own language. They have said things that no one has yet repeated more eloquently nor more concisely. They combine to form the ultimate yardstick by which all other literatures are measured. 'There are types of education', said Lucian, 'less paying than the commercial, yet better worth paying for . . .'.

The Roman road at Trelleck led to a narrow avenue of trees, through which I looked down on a green valley chequered with pink ploughland. If, like myself, you have spent most of your life among hills, a level landscape seems tame. It may, of course, be a beautiful landscape. It may cradle memorable buildings, majestic rivers, historic associations; yet to hillfolk it will always lack that aura of challenge and that rhythm of undulation which are found only on the heights. Presently the trees fell astern, revealing the River Wye and a hillside hamlet called Llandogo. John Bloomfield, an eighteenth-century Suffolk peasant, set the scene simply:

> The air resigned its hazy blue
> Just as Llandogo came in view,
> Delightful village; one by one
> Its climbing dwellings caught the sun.
> So bright the scene, the air so clear,
> Young Love and Joy seemed stationed here.

If Joy and Young Love are still stationed at Llandogo, they will need to shout above the summer traffic on a main road opposite Tintern Abbey, which Lord Houghton rated as 'this noble argosy of faith'. When Wordsworth revisited Tintern, after an interval of five years, he found the scene as beautiful as ever:

> Once again
> Do I behold these steep and lofty cliffs,
> That on a wild secluded scene impress
> Thoughts of more deep seclusion; and connect
> The landscape with the quiet of the sky.

It was in 1131 that Walter de Clare, Lord of Chepstow, founded an abbey beside the River Wye at Tintern, on a site so wild and so remote that only the sheep-farming Cistercians could have cultivated it, and only because they enlisted a large number of peasants as lay brothers. Scarcely anything of the first foundation has survived. The present ruins are those of a thirteenth-century abbey whose precincts covered twenty-seven acres. Soon after the Dissolution the abbey roof was removed, and the King's plumbers received £8 for melting the lead. In 1756 the ruins were preserved by the Beaufort family. In 1847 a tentative excavation was begun. In 1900 the abbey and several thousand adjacent acres were bought by the Crown. Today we have the shell of a cruciform church, seventy-five yards long and fifty yards broad, together with fragments of the monks' common room, book room, infirmary, refectory, kitchen, and chapter house.

Of all our abbeys, Tintern is the most gloriously sited, in the middle of a wide and curving valley. The glassless windows frame a landscape of grazing sheep and lofty summits, best viewed from Tintern's hillside parish church, a thirteenth-century building with a saddleback belfry. As at Oxford and Cambridge, you must visit Tintern in winter, or late on an evening in May, when the moon strokes the walls with silent finger. Then you will see the vision that granted to Wordsworth a brief respite,

In which the heavy and the weary weight
Of all this unintelligible world
Is lightened.

Tintern's moonlit *Ichabod* made a memorable finale to my journey through the Marches.

9 THE SOUTH WEST

I reached the South West at a point near Bristol, where the last
of the Marches yielded to the first of the factories. Formerly a
handsome town and the chief harbour west of London, Bristol
still contains a few traces of dignity and beauty, but they shine
like currants in a duff of industry, commerce, suburbs and roads
covering an area so vast that to walk round it would take several
days. The men who 'developed' Bristol deserve the epitaph
which Dr Abel Evans wrote for Sir John Vanburgh:

> Lie heavy on him, earth, for he
> Laid many a heavy load on thee.

Soon after leaving Bristol, I sighted the Mendip Hills, whose
summits are solitary and rewarding. The range stretches from
the edge of Weston-super-Mare to the edge of Frome, about
twenty-five miles away. The highest point, Black Down, is more
than a thousand feet above the sea. The villages are few and
small: Priddy, for example, whose sheep fair was so important
that in 1352 the village became the first place in Somerset to hear
a formal reading of a new Weights and Measures Act. The old
hurdle-stick on Priddy Green recalls the importance of sheep.
Oldest of all are Priddy Barrows, a cluster of prehistoric burial
sites. Another village, Charterhouse-on-Mendip, was named
after a thirteenth-century *Chartreuse* or monastery which the
Carthusians built among hills that are always rugged and often
bleak. From Manor Farm a lane reaches a derelict lead-mining
region which the Romans exploited. They built a road from the
mines, joining the Celtic Harrow Way across Salisbury Plain via
Kilmington and Amesbury. A mound near some crossroads
marks the site of an amphitheatre or sports arena for the soldiers
who guarded and supervised the mines. What a nation the

Romans were! From the Devonshire coast to the Perthshire braes they imprinted the outward and visible signs of an inward and comfortable civilisation.

I shall pass over in silence the roar of traffic that harried me into Bridgwater, an industrial and therefore ugly place, though once a pleasant town and inland harbour, home of Robert Blake, the seventeenth-century admiral, who declared: 'I would have the whole world know that none save an Englishman shall chastise an Englishman'. Were he alive today, the admiral would think twice before trusting his passport eastward of Clacton Pier.

From the suburbs of Bridgwater you can within five minutes reach the Quantocks, the most beautiful small range of hills in Britain, scarcely five miles wide and less than fifteen miles long. Within that narrow compass you have moors, woods, seascapes, cornfields, pastures, streams and many sandstone houses. My own favourite hamlet is Aisholt (Old English *aescholt* or 'ash copse'), a Thankful Village, so-called because all of its Servicemen returned alive from World War I. There are only thirty-two such villages in England, of which Somerset contains seven, the largest number in any county. Aisholt comprises a church and a few cottages set beside a lane that dips into a wooded combe. Coleridge wished to make his home in this deep seclusion, but his wife did not. A later poet, Sir Henry Newbolt, was more fortunate. He did make his home at Aisholt, in a cottage which Lady Newbolt had inherited. 'I hope,' he said, 'that no one will ever spread the fame of Aisholt.' I would have respected Newbolt's wishes, had not tourism long ago transformed the Quantocks into a holiday resort.

Crowcombe lies at the foot of the Quantocks. The approach from Nether Stowey may well be the steepest in England, for the gradient tugs at your calf-muscles, and the banks are so high that you gaze up at the roots of trees. A twelfth-century lord of the manor, Godfrey de Crowcombe, witnessed the Magna Carta ceremony at Runnymede in 1215. This small place was once a borough with a market cross where people met to do business, to talk politics, to swap scandal, and sometimes to remember that they lived under the eye of Calvary. Crowcombe's church of the Holy Cross bears an uncommon dedication; its highboxed family pew was designed for Crowcombe Court in the years before the house became an hotel. The most interesting feature of the village is a twelfth-century church house which for many years served as a school-cum-almshouse, and is now the village hall.

Unlike Crowcombe, which lies in a hollow, Broomfield stands on high moorland, whence its ancient name *Brunfella* or 'broom-covered open country'. Perhaps that is why Collinson's *History of Somerset* stated: 'This parish has always been remarkably healthy, even in times of general sickness elsewhere'. The church contains some notable wood carving and a memorial to Mrs F. A. M. Coombe who 'by her last will and testament left money to provide a dinner of roast beef and plum pudding with bread and vegetables in sufficient quantity, and a pint of beer for 6 poor men and 6 poor women'. Like Kirkharle and Capheaton, Broomfield bred a celebrity, Andrew Cross, who was born at Fynes Court in 1784. The house had belonged to his family since the sixteenth century, but was destroyed by fire in 1908. Cross, at all events, installed a laboratory of scientific paraphernalia, chiefly of the electrical or shocking sort. Being a classical scholar as well as magnetic fielder, he attached to each of his dangerous devices a card bearing the words *Noli Me Tangere* (Do Not Touch Me). The servants, who were not classical scholars, had sometimes to learn Latin by experience. Several of Cross's electrifications were described in the *Proceedings* of the British Association. He so loved Broomfield that he spent his whole life there, dying in the room where he had been born.

The Quantocks contain a village, Nether Stowey, and a hamlet, Holford, which are writ large on the map of English poetry. At Nether Stowey stands the house which Thomas Poole, a local tanner, lent to Coleridge who lived there for several years, a victim of drugs and matrimony. His presence in that place at that time made possible one of the most fruitful friendships in our literature. We do not know when Coleridge first saw Wordsworth, but we do know that in 1797 both men were living in Somerset. Very likely they met while visiting their publisher, Cottle, at Bristol. The point is, Wordsworth and his sister stayed with Coleridge at Nether Stowey, whence they walked to Holford, not far from the sea at East Quantoxhead. Dorothy Wordsworth was enchanted by Holford: 'There is everything here,' she wrote, 'sea, woods, wild as fancy ever painted, brooks clear and pebbly as in Cumberland . . .'. To Thomas Poole she confessed her dream of finding a Holford cottage at a small rent. Within a week the generous Poole had arranged that the Wordsworths should indeed pay a small rent at Holford, not for a cottage, but for a Queen Anne mansion, called variously Alfoxden and Alfoxton. So, the two poets formed a famous friendship.

Holford lies along a lane that has not greatly changed since Wordsworth remembered the days when

> Upon smooth Quantocks' airy ridge we roved
> Unchecked . . .

Hidden among trees, the gable-tower church displays a list of rectors since 1319. As a token of gratitude, a plaque records the fact that Wellington House, a boys' preparatory school, moved to Holford during World War II. When egalitarian vandals wrecked the plaque, the school repaired it: 'At the invitation of the Rector and his parishioners the School has replaced it here in witness of its faith and in memory of its seven years among the people of Holford'. Beyond the church, the lane becomes a track climbing past some cottages and so to a greensward beside one of Dorothy's 'brooks clear and pebbly as in Cumberland'. Then the track becomes a path through a wood to the summit of a grassy plateau which may be the very place where Wordsworth roved unchecked.

From Holford the Wordsworths and Coleridge walked to Lynmouth and back, a stroll of seventy miles. Being poets and therefore poor, they proposed to cover the cost of their journey by together writing a poem for the *New Monthly Magazine*. The poem was duly written, but not with Wordsworth's help, for it was called 'The Rime of the Ancient Mariner' and Coleridge began it when the trio sighted Watchet harbour:

> The ship was cheered, the harbour cleared,
> Merrily did we drop
> Below the hill, below the kirk,
> Below the lighthouse top.

From that poem a real co-operation did arise, the *Lyrical Ballads*, which tried to avoid what Wordsworth called 'the gaudiness and inane phraseology' of a jaded Augustan style. The new generation of poets, he declared, would take all experience as their theme: 'The remotest discoveries of the Chemist, the Botanist, or Minerologist will be as proper objects of the Poet's art as are any upon which it can be employed'. But let us not forget Dorothy. Wordsworth at least did not forget:

> She, in the midst of all, preserved me still
> A Poet, made me seek beneath that name
> My office upon earth . . .

Modern insight perceives that the bond between brother and sister was incestuous albeit sublimated and 'innocent'. Wordsworth himself broke free, and married happily for life; but Dorothy collapsed under a strain which ended in dementia. Nevertheless, her *Alfoxden Journal* set the Quantock scene vividly: 'A mild morning with windows open at breakfast, and the redbreasts singing in the garden. Walked with Coleridge over the hills. The sea at first appeared obscured by vapour; that vapour soon afterwards slid into one mighty mass along the seashore . . . I never saw such a union of earth, sky, and sea . . . Gathered sticks in the woods; perfect stillness. Of a great number of sheep in the field, only one standing. Returned to dinner at five o'clock. The moonlight still as warm as a summer night . . .'. There with one voice spoke Martha and Mary, the domestic diary and a poet's vision. No wonder Wordsworth said:

> She gave me eyes, she gave me ears.

Cothelstone lies on the Quantock's western perimeter. Two centuries ago Collinson claimed that the view from Cothelstone Beacon revealed 'fourteen counties, and with a glass on a clear day, 150 churches'. I was content to sight my next destination, the Brendon Hills, rising from a vale as green and as pink as at Llandogo. It would be a long time before I sighted many more furrows, because the route crossed a country too wild and wet for wheat.

Cothelstone hamlet, at the foot of the Beacon, can be reached only by following a track under a sandstone arch. Then you find some cottages, a church, a farm and a manor house which for

seven centuries was the seat of the Stawell family. Sir John
Stawell held it for King Charles against the rebels, who
ultimately captured him, burned his house, felled his woods, and
sold his lands. Sir John's son was created Lord Stawell by
Charles II.

Beyond Cothelstone I approached the western border of
Saxon England. What lay beyond—Exmoor, Dartmoor,
Cornwall—was so distant and inclement that it failed to attract
the early waves of Saxon invaders. The number and nature of
placenames show that Devon during the seventh century AD was
a sparsely populated Celtic region. Somerset, on the other hand,
was the land of the *Sumorton-saete* or 'dwellers at and near
Somerton', a small town which calls itself the Capital of Wessex,
basing that claim on a local man, Ine or Ina, who in 688 was
elected King of Wessex. Something more than poetic licence
inspired the old song, 'The Green Hills of Somerset', for the
county includes the Mendips, Poldens, Quantocks, Brendons,
and part of Exmoor. Somerset has its own sea, the Severn Sea or
Bristol Channel, leading to the Atlantic. It has Wells Cathedral,
with the noblest west front in Britain. It has Bath, the *locus
classicus* of English domestic architecture. It has three notable
schools . . . Kingswood, Bruton, Monkton Combe. It has the
finest church towers in the kingdom, and from Dulverton to
Castle Cary a chain of handsome little towns.

Bishops Lydeard belonged to the Bishops of Wells. It stands a
mile or more from Cothelstone, and was a charming place until
Taunton co-opted it as a suburb. Flanked by a high wall, the
lane from the village curved among trees, crossed the main road
to Minehead, dived under the bridge of a vanished railway, and
then began a fifteen-mile journey across the Brendons, entering
neither village nor hamlet, and passing so few houses that, after
many journeys, I knew them all by heart. The ascent started
near Elworthy, the entry to the Exmoor National Park. For
nearly a mile the road was a steeply twisting avenue; then the
trees thinned, the summit appeared, and the Quantocks were
seen astern, wooded, pastured, pink-furrowed.

Continuing along the spine of the Brendons, I caught sight of
the sea, shining like blue silk. Beyond it the Welsh coast was so
clear that some of its white buildings could be seen; but not, alas,

the ships which used to ply from shore to shore. Only one small coaster appeared, recalling the words of the Ancient Mariner:

As idle as a painted ship
Upon a painted ocean.

Still the road went its secluded way, as though in search of a house. After a few miles it found one, a lonely inn at Raleighs Cross. Just beyond the inn, on the left, a track led to Tripp Farm and thence down a couple of steep meadows to Clatworthy Reservoir, where a Cornishman might have imagined himself beside the River Fal. The hills were thick with oak and ash that came down to the water, and the water curved out of sight among interlocking spurs, and on it a dinghy was tethered. Two cuckoos sounded like four while their serenade ran round the valley.

Returning to the road, I soon reached a chapel as lonely as the inn. It was an ugly yet a pious place, shining like a good deed in a sparsely populated world. Many of the nineteenth-century worshippers had to walk several miles to the Sunday service. This chapel was one of Wesley's legacies, built partly as a political club and partly as a pathway to Paradise. As we observed at Epworth, Wesley himself wished to revive the Church of England, but his followers decided to forsake it. Wesley's revivalism reaped its richest harvest in the south-west. Devon and Cornwall, in fact, built more chapels per thousand people than did any other county. A moving tribute to these simple Bethels was paid by Elihu Burritt, the American whom we met in the Border Region. Burritt informed his fellowcountrymen that 'by travelling over a space of three centuries' breadth, they will see . . . the houses in which the first settlers in New England were born; the churches and chapels in which they were baptised, and the school-houses in which they learned the alphabet of the great language that is to fill the earth with the speech of man's rights . . .'. How well he spoke for both nations: 'One hundred millions, speaking the tongue of Shakespeare and Milton on the American continent . . . shall moor their memories to these humble dwellings of England's hamlets, and feel how many taut and twisted liens attach them to the motherland of mighty nations'. The statistics of tourism

prove that Burritt's words are as true today as when he wrote
them.

Still the Severn Sea and the Welsh hills shone between wind-
bent beeches; still no village appeared, and only such houses as
could withstand snow, rain, gales. If a summit hereabout is less
than eight hundred feet high you tend to look down on it; if less
than five hundred feet, you regard it as part of the valley. The
Brendons' medieval name was *Brundon* (Old English *brun dun* or
'brown hill'), which suggests that the summits were then a waste
of bracken and heather, like the wild tracts of Exmoor today.
Although the month was June, and the weather brilliant, I met
only one car between Elworthy and the lonely chapel. It was like
driving on a private road through a semi-mountainous estate.
How different, I thought, from Kent's domesticated Garden of
England, from sandy Bagshot Heath, courtly Windsor, and the
gentle Vale of Aylesbury; even more different from the Fens;
different, too, from the hills above Clun and from those other
hills above Tintern; different in ways which elude the grasp of
language; different in appearance, in history, in dialect and
architecture and climate; different, finally, from those many
places which lay beyond my route . . . those homely Essex
villages near Constable's mill in Suffolk, those Leicestershire
hedgerows made-to-measure for huntsmen, those islands of
agriculture in Staffordshire's industrial Sargasso, those
comparable islands in Lamb's beloved Hertfordshire, and, not
least, those deep countrysides of North Buckinghamshire where
as a child I introduced myself to rural England.

Mendips, Quantocks, Brendons; and now at last Exmoor,
seen afar as a green and heathery switchback on the sky. The
name 'Exmoor' does not appear on the Ordnance maps. What
you find is 'Exmoor Forest', anciently a royal chase containing
only two trees, Kite Oak and Hoar Oak. The boundaries of the
medieval forest were clearly defined, occasionally altered, and
periodically patrolled; but the district is nowadays conveniently
classified as that within the Exmoor National Park, extending
from Elworthy in Somerset to Combe Martin in Devon, and
southward to Dulverton in Somerset. The wild tracts are best
seen between Cloutsham and the North Devon coast near
Hunter's Inn, where the cliffs create a rampart that awed

Charles Kingsley: 'What a seawall they are, those Exmoor hills! Sheer upward from the sea a thousand feet'. The loneliest and bleakest zone is The Chains in Devon. John Leland found nothing good to say of Exmoor when he crossed it four centuries ago: 'Forest, barren and Morish ground where is store and breading of young Catelle, but little or no Corne or habitation'.

Two men were chiefly responsible for reclaiming parts of Exmoor. The first, James Boevey, a seventeenth-century Dutch emigre, was an irascible and litigious person who acquired land near Simonsbath in Somerset, at a time when a government survey repeated Leland's denigration by saying 'the said Chace is a mountainous and cold Ground, very sorie sheepe pasture, overgrown Heath . . a poore kind of Turfe of little value'. Despite many setbacks and mistakes, Boevey managed to reclaim some of the moor and to build a large house at Simonsbath, parts of which may be seen in the hotel on the site. Two centuries later came the Knights, a family of Midland industrialists, who not only extended Boevey's work but also built several roads and farmhouses. Their ultimate ambition—to transform the moor into a mining area—remains unfulfilled.

The road across the Brendons does at last reach a village at Wheddon Cross which lies in a hollow, dominated by what Jan Ridd's servant called 'the haighest place of Hexmoor', that is, Dunkery Beacon, nearly 1,800 feet above the sea. Jan himself once watched Dunkery from his snowbound farm while rumour spread as fast as the flames that generated it: 'The Doones are firing Dunkery beacon, to celebrate their new captain'. When Queen Victoria celebrated her Jubilee, forty-four beacon fires were sighted from Dunkery. When I arrived, however, the only fiery spectacle was the sun. Northward the Welsh hills shone like a humpbacked meadow dotted with mushrooms that were white buildings. In the middle distance the land fell away and then swooped up again, crowned with woods. Southward stood the Quantocks and the Brendons, beyond them, the Worcestershire Beacon at Malvern. No other Westcountry summit offers such a wide and varied vista.

Despite encroachment by farmers and foresters, Exmoor remains unspoiled. It possesses no commercial attractions for the tourist; many of its lanes deter the motorist; and the wildest tracts can be reached only on foot or astride a horse. My own route brought me to my home in the Devon sector of the moor, several miles from a village. Standing on the brow above one of my small fields I saw sheep grazing at sixteen hundred feet among the larks. From a lower field I watched two stags ambling across the opposite hill. By turning about, from east to west, I saw Dartmoor, Devon's other vast solitude. Dartmoor is not a duplicate of Exmoor. It is larger, bleaker, and far more popular with tourists. More than a century ago Kingsley deplored the invasion: 'of that noble moorland range so much had been said and sung of late, I am afraid it is becoming somewhat cockney and trite'. Exmoor's climate is always bracing and sometimes boisterous, but never so wet and misty as on Dartmoor. Each of the moors has its own breed of ponies, its own ancient rights and obligations, its own history of mining; but whereas Exmoor is no longer Crown land, Dartmoor has for centuries formed part of the Duchy of Cornwall, an appanage of the Sovereign's eldest son, the Prince of Wales. Each moor has its own niche in literature. Thus, Dartmoor's chief spokesmen were a twentieth-century novelist, Eden Phillpotts, and an eighteenth-century poet, Noel Barrington, who emphasised Dartmoor's barren solitude:

> Thy rugged hills
> Have seldom echoed with the peasant's voice
> Inspiring his patient team.

Exmoor's spokesman was Richard Doddridge Blackmore, whose *Lorna Doone* distils the substance and spirit of the moor, and the lives and legends of its people. Exmoor received an unsolicited testimonial from a Kentish poet, Vita Sackville-West: 'This,' she said, 'is the England one would wish to show the foreigner—quiet, withdrawn, rather poor, but rich in love and tradition'.

On Exmoor I halted and refused to go any further, not from weariness nor cussedness, but because the holiday season had at last overtaken my leisurely progress, and I was unwilling to see the South West at its worst, a victim of what Dr J. A. Williamson called 'the sale of a country's charms for money, a species of harlotry'.

For three months I waited, safe in my eyrie, defended by steep lanes whose narrow deviousness causes the car-conscious visitor either to avoid them or, having ventured, to put back, dented and scratched, vowing never again to enter such outposts of feudalism. My retreat, however, was not a gesture of defeat; it was a respite *pour mieux sauter*; and while it lasted I acquired a bird's eye view of Devon, the land of the *Dumnonii*, which the Welsh called *Dyfnaint*. Devon is by general consent the most beautiful county in England. Practical persons, not given to linguistic analysis, call it 'Glorious Devon'. Since Yorkshire and Lincolnshire are both trisected into administrative regions, Devon is the largest undivided English county, covering more than 2,610 square miles, yet having a population of less than a million, most of whom live in Exeter, Plymouth and Torquay. Devon's south coast is as mild as Cornwall's; the north coast is taller and more varied. Devon is the highest county south of the Pennines, standing on average 1,200 feet above the sea, topped by two hundred tors, some of which exceed 2,000 feet and are therefore mountains. Devon contains three hundred square miles of almost treeless moorland; 80,000 acres of woods; and pastures so rich they nurture the finest cattle in southern England, the Devon Red Rubies of the South Hams. More than any other county, Devon is a nursery of seamen: Sir Francis Drake, Sir Walter Raleigh, Sir Richard Grenville, Sir John Hawkins, Sir Humphrey Gilbert, John Davies, John Oxenham, Stephen Borough. Truly the men of Devon have obeyed the signal which the Admiralty made in 1661: 'It is with His Majesty's Navies, Ships of War, and forces at sea . . . that the Wealth, Safety, and Strength of this Kingdom is so much concerned'. Devon answers to a roll call of writers who were either natives or long-established residents: John Gay of Barnstaple, Charles Kingsley of Westward Ho!, Coleridge of Ottery St. Mary, John Ford of Ilsington, Robert Herrick of Dean Prior, Anthony Froude of Dartington, Robert Stephen Hawker of Stoke Damerel, William Browne of Tavistock, Sabine Baring-Gould of Lew Trenchard, R. D. Blackmore of Exmoor, Eden Phillpotts of Dartmoor. Quoting from memory, I recall Sir Thomas Bodley (greatest of all English librarians) and Richard Hooker (clerical politician) both born at Exeter; Henry de Bracton (medieval jurist), born at

Bracton or Bratton Fleming; General Monk (restorer of Charles II), born at Merton; Captain Scott (of the Antarctic), born at Plymouth; Archbishop William Temple, born at Culmstock. Surveying his kith and kin, a Devon man may say with Stephen Spender:

I think continually of those who were truly great . . .

Meantime, the summer waned while I waited for the traffic to do likewise. But had I waited too long? Would the last lap of my journey evoke an autumnal elegy instead of a perennial *sursum corda*? The first morning in September awoke to a mist that was soon joined by a drizzle which lasted all night and far into the next day. Then, like a benign bolt from the blue, the third morning dawned so fresh and sunny that even a countryman might have mistaken it for June. It was the kind of day on which Enoch Arden

Like a lover down thro' all his blood
Drew in the dewy early-morning breath
Of England . . .

Soon after seven o'clock I was ambling at twenty miles an hour through a maze of lanes to Barnstaple, the oldest borough in Britain, with a charter of AD 930. Barnstaple Grammar School nurtured two famous men, Bishop Jewel (author of *A Defence of the Church of England*) and John Gay (author of *The Beggar's Opera*). Modern Barnstaple is a dreary amalgam of light industry and heavy traffic. The few oases of beauty and quietude include two seventeenth-century almshouses, Penrose's and Horwood's. On market days the pannier market sells large brown eggs, homemade jam, homebaked scones, and other wares from cottages and farms.

The road from Barnstaple to Bideford overlooks the Torridge Estuary, but is itself overlooked by an almost unbroken chain of new houses. I therefore followed the old road, a twisting lane; and at the end of it I entered Bideford, a relatively unspoiled inland harbour, whence sailed Stephen and William Borough in a small pinnace called the *Spendthrift*, God-speeded by Sebastian Cabot, then eighty years of age. Down the Torridge they went, across the Bar, into the Severn Sea and so to Russia, the first

177

English vessel ever to reach that country. From the same port sailed Sir Richard Grenville in the *Revenge*, never to return, for he engaged a Spanish fleet, one ship against many, fighting from sunset until midnight, receiving eight hundred direct hits. When most of his crew were dead, and all the survivors wounded, Grenville ordered the carpenter to blow up the ship rather than surrender; but his brave crew begged to be allowed to return to their families, whereupon Grenville relented, and did strike his flag, soon afterwards dying of wounds. His last words will outlive the men who mock them: 'Here die I, Richard Grenville, with a joyful and quiet mind, for that I have ended my life as a true soldier ought to do, that hath fought for his country, his queen, religion, and honour . . .'.

The landscape west of Bideford may appear unimpressive to a traveller who has lately seen Exmoor, and is about to see Hartland. If, however, the traveller avoids the main roads by following the lanes via Landcross, Fairy Cross, and Bradworthy, he will agree that their profound seclusion goes some way toward compensating for a lack of spectacular vistas. He will certainly not be disappointed by Welcombe, a remote hamlet near the sea, where he will find a church with Norman tower, Jacobean lectern, and the oldest timber screen in Devon. He will find, too, a holy well and a few cottages, but not much else, unless it be a motorist marooned in the labyrinth of lanes and tracks and towering rhododendrons.

A few hundred yards south-west from Welcombe I entered Cornwall, the most romantic county in Britain, if by 'romance' is meant rugged seascapes, desolate moorlands, sub-tropical gardens, heroic legends, Celtic lineage, and a halo of saintly placenames. Cornwall was called *Cornubia*, a corruption of *Cornovii*, a Celtic tribe. The Old English *Cornwealas* means 'the Welsh in Cornwall'. Here the Celts took their last stand against the Romans and all other invaders who crossed the River Tamar. It is therefore a fact, not a fantasy, that many Cornishfolk are descended from tribes whom we describe as Celtic. Beatrix Potter noted the social characteristics in 1892: 'The people here are all singularly alike, and one can well believe that they are the purest race in Britain . . . very friendly, kindly, cheerful . . .'. The dark-skinned Cornishfolk resemble their

Celtic cousins not only in Wales and Scotland but also in Spain (Matthew Arnold's 'dark Iberians'). In short, the Celtic genes have not yet been wholly diluted by marriage with persons of Germanic or Scandinavian ancestry.

Cornwall's most eloquent spokesman was Sir Arthur Quiller-Couch, poet, essayist, novelist, scholar, sailor. Q (as he signed himself) graduated at Oxford, and became Professor of English Literature at Cambridge, being also Mayor of Fowey, where he lived for many years. Q stood to Cornwall as Hardy to Wessex and as Wordsworth to Lakeland; a native, a critic, an interpreter. Not to have read his Cornish books is to remain partly unaware of what Cornwall was like within living memory. Q lived long to witness the debasement of Cornwall into a holiday playground. 'Hideous hotels', he complained, 'thrust themselves insistently on my sight as I walk on magnificent cliffs . . . .'. My father spent some of his childhood in Cornwall during the 1880s, with a brother and sister who were born there, from all of whom I learned much of that magical land at that leisurely time. Even during my own childhood the county was lit by the final flicker of a departing glory. To make the point once again, agriculture is no longer the largest employer of labour; on the contrary, our farmland dwindles by tens of thousands of acres every year while one machine performs the work of twenty men. Moreover, almost every adult now enjoys several weeks of annual holidaymaking, and the majority of families own at least one car. So, events have fulfilled the prediction that was made by *The Cornish Magazine* a century ago: 'Unless Cornishmen look to it, their country will be spoiled before they know it'.

Morwenstow is Cornwall's most northerly parish, perched near the Atlantic coast, sometimes lulled and sometimes deafened by rollers eternally obeying Tennyson's command:

Break, break, break
On thy cold, gray stones, O Sea.

The cliffs at Morwenstow are so tall that the mind grows dizzy gazing down at the waves. Many of the coves cannot be reached except from the sea. In the days of sail the coast westward to Land's End was dubbed 'The Sailor's Graveyard'. The best parts of Morwenstow lie within a few hundreds of the sea, where the church, the vicarage, and a cottage form an ecumenical trinity. The village was raised from obscurity by one of its Victorian vicars, Robert Stephen Hawker, an eccentric poet. His first wife (young enough to be his mother) taught at the village school which Hawker had built. He designed also the vicarage (now a private residence) in a hollow near the church, part of the graveyard being reserved for the burial of those who had been shipwrecked on the coast. Hawker wrote many books and poems about Cornwall, including the oft-quoted 'And shall Trelawny die?' As an elderly widower, addicted to laudanum, he married a Roman Catholic girl (young enough to be his daughter) who, it is said, persuaded him to make a deathbed submission to Rome. Hawker's most durable monument may be the Harvest Festival, a form of fruitful thanksgiving which he devised at Morwenstow. Some of his fellow-clergy dismissed the festival as Popery, but, within a few years of his death the service was common throughout England.

A public footpath follows the coast, haunted by Thomas Hardy, son of a Dorset stonemason, who—as an architect's assistant—was sent to restore the church at St Juliot near Boscastle, a parish without a village, where one of Hardy's sketches hangs from the church wall. Hardy was received by the vicar's sister, with whom he made a marriage that was foredoomed because the wife never came to terms with the melancholy temperament and humble origins of her anti-Christian husband. In the end she went mad, a fact for which Hardy felt partly responsible. In a novel called *A Pair of Blue Eyes* he idealised his courtship, and continued to idealise it until he died. Neither the years nor a second marriage could dispel his remorseful nostalgia. As an old man he returned to St Juliot and fancied that he saw his fiancée—'the very west of Wessex girl'—walking beside a pony. Then the phantom receded:

> I look back at it amid the rain
> For the very last time; for my sand is sinking,
> And I shall traverse love's old domain
> Never again.

From Beeny Head (the subject of another of Hardy's nostalgic poems) I glanced westward to Tintagel, an Arthurian site and therefore controversial. The stories about King Arthur are so tall that one doubts whether they convinced even the inventors of them (the chief yarn-spinner being Geoffrey of Monmouth, a twelfth-century Welsh bishop). Cornwall is littered with Arthurian legends. Camelford, they say, was Camelot, the scene of Arthur's last battle. His sword, Excalibur, was cast into a Cornish pool (some say near Helston; others on Bodmin Moor). At St Kew he built two castles; at Tintagel he held his Round Table conferences; at Warbstow he was buried. Somerset, however, claims that he was buried at Glastonbury, and that Cadbury, not Camelford, was Camelot. The Welsh, for their part, affirm that Arthur was one of themselves. His Table or *Bwrdd* stood at Anglesey; his coronation took place at Caerleon; his body was buried at Craig-y-Dinas.

Arthur is not mentioned by any of his contemporaries; only in the ninth century did Nennius write *Historia Brittonum,* citing several traditions about a warrior who defeated the Saxons at the Badonic Hill. From those traditions the Arthurian Cycle proliferated down the centuries, with additions from Malory to Masefield; all praising the Flower of Kings (*Flos Regum Arturus*) who would rise again and once more save his people, as foretold by Tennyson:

He passes to be King among the dead,
And after healing of his grievous wound
He comes again . . .

Although the round table and the magic sword may be dismissed as fairytales, it seems unlikely that the Arthurian legend could have flourished without some foundation in fact. Hereward the Wake and Bold Robin Hood had each his living prototype. R. G. Collingwood, the eminent historian, said of Arthur: 'The historicity of the man can hardly be called in question'.

Few people will claim that the north of Cornwall is more beautiful than the south. Fewer still will deny that the north is more spectacular, if only because the Atlantic out-rolls the Channel. I had a special reason for revisiting south Cornwall, because for several years I lived in a boat near St Anthony-in-Roseland, across the bay from Falmouth. In order to reach my old anchorage I now headed toward Bodmin Moor, dominated by Brown Willy, 1375 feet above the sea, the summit of a granite range extending to Land's End. In clear weather the peak reveals Dartmoor, the Atlantic, and miles of rough pasture studded with stone walls and winding tracks. Margaret Leigh, who farmed on Bodmin Moor said: 'On the moor there are few days in the year when no wind blows'. During a full gale, she added, 'uproar fills the world, in the midst of which the worker, cut off from his kind by a barrier of noise, walks alone, unhearing and unheard. Everything movable is in motion, clanging and banging, flapping and rattling'.

Bodmin itself—formerly the county town—retains some agreeable nooks and crannies, and an impressively wide main street; but at Bugle and St Austell the sky is gashed by ersatz Alps, the debris from a local china clay industry. Mining and other activities have wrought a comparable havoc at Camborne and Redruth.

Soon after leaving St Austell, the main road sends a lane southward into Roseland, the most beautiful region of Cornwall; so beautiful that many visitors misinterpret its name, which does not connote roses, but comes from the Cornish *ros* ('wild' or 'healthy'), an apt description of the region in the years before it was cultivated. Roseland is a vague area. Some people say that it forms a triangle, with Truro as apex and with Veryan and Falmouth as bases; others say that it consists of two narrow peninsulas which end respectively at St Mawes and Zone Point. The remotest and most spectacular sector extends from St Gerrans to Zone Point, a distance of about three miles. Parts of it still recall the untamed *ros*. There are a few houses and farms on this peninsula, as well as the church of St Anthony-in-Roseland (a parish without a village) and Place house (formerly the seat of the Spry family). One side of the peninsula overlooks the Channel and several sandy beaches; the other side overlooks Percuil River flowing between wooded hills. Below Percuil you reach St Mawes which rises like a Mediterranean fishing village, tier upon tier of coloured houses, some white, some pink, some blue, or yellow, or green. In my father's childhood St Mawes

182

really was a fishing village; now it is a holiday resort and last home of the rich. Further yet lie Falmouth and its docks, and the River Fal leading to Truro. Furthest of all, you sight the wooded banks of Helford River, where Q dropped anchor:

All the wood to ransack,
All the wave explore—
Moon on Calamansack,
Ripple on the shore.

Helford River was to Q as Percuil River was to me; a haven of magical delight, drenched green and blue when the sun rose; etched black and white when the moon silvered the water, and my boat creaked in her sleepless meditation.

Less than twelve miles from Helford stands Lizard Point, the southernmost tip of England, a region of gorse-gold heathland and cavernous cliffs. Francis Kilvert set the scene in 1871: 'The coast became very wild and timber almost disappeared. Along the roadsides grew large bushes of beautiful heather, white, pink and rose colour, growing freely as gorse . . . I never saw anything like the wonderful colour of the serpentine rocks, rich, deep, warm, variegated, mottled and streaked and vein red, green and white'. This stone is made into ornaments by craftsmen at Lizard Town, a small clifftop village, the Cornish *lis ard* or 'High place'. Ten miles offshore lie the dreaded Manacles, seeking whom they may devour. Cornwall's Atlantic coast has claimed the greater number of vessels, but this sector of the Channel coast has claimed the greater number of lives, chiefly because the wrecked ships were larger than those that foundered off the north coast. Whenever a mist shrouds these parts the Lizard lighthouse sounds a bitternlike foghorn.

East and west of Lizard Town the coast offers many coves and miniature harbours at Kynance, Mullion, Cadgwith, Coverack, Porthleven, Gunwalloe.

The further west you travel, the deeper grows your awareness of the Celtic dawn that became a twilight. Severe historians may protest that the awareness is spurious because fanciful, yet the fact remains, the Celts did retreat westward, and in these parts their relics do abound, notably at the prehistoric village on a hill at Chysauster near Penzance. As late as the sixteenth century a topographer described Cornwall as 'a foreign country on that side of England next to Spain'. It is true, also, that at the beginning of this century the elderly Cornishfolk described as 'foreigner' any visitor from across the Tamar; the same word was sometimes applied to natives of East Cornwall. There is therefore some truth in the old maxim: 'East of Truro, out of Cornwall'. During the 1960s Claude Berry could still say: 'Sitting in a restaurant in Truro, or listening to the talk in the streets on a market day, I think I can tell fairly accurately who comes from the West, and from Mid and East Cornwall'.

Two miles short of Marazion I met a harvester who said: 'The glass is high, but 'tis starting to wobble. You'm safe till suppertime, though I'd not bank on the weather holding after nightfall'.

Accelerating from twenty-five to thirty miles an hour, I sighted St Michael's Mount, reputedly a relic of Lyonesse, King Arthur's kingdom, long since sunk beneath the sand. The islet is crowned by a castle—Milton's 'great vision of the guarded isle'—occupied by the descendants of its ancient lords, the Saint Aubyn family.

Penzance, the last town on my journey, is the *pen sant* or 'holy headland' that was razed by the Spaniards in 1595. Little of the first rebuilding has survived. The best parts of the town are late Georgian; the worst, post-1850. Penzance harbour has been rescued from redundancy by pleasure craft, Trinity House vessels, and a ferry to the Scilly Isles. The public gardens above the harbour contain sub-tropical plants that bloom throughout the year. Hearing a clock strike two, I glanced up at the cloudless sky, and was surprised that I had so nearly reached my ultimate destination. Like life itself, the journey at its beginning had seemed infinite, or at any rate so long that the end appeared remote; but now, like life itself, the journey had overtaken me and the pursuer was himself pursued. How distant seemed my setting-out from Dover; how distant those sunny hours on Romney Marsh, and the sight of Windsor Castle overlooking the Thames that led toward the Chilterns. How far off in time and place seemed Pastor Moritz's Oxford ('the most beautiful city in the world'), and Cambridge's waterside colleges, and Wesley's Fenland curacy at Wroot, and Wordsworth's cottage at

Grasmere. Faintest of all was Flodden Field and the Scottish border at Coldstream.

Immersed in those traveller's tales, I soon outflanked Mount's Bay, and reached Mousehole alias Mowzel, anciently called St Enys, which in 1595 shared the fiery fate of Penzance. Here the houses climbed from small harbour to a steep cliff top. The narrow street zig-zagged quietly, except when someone clattered across the cobbles of an alley. The summer crowds had departed, leaving Mousehole to transform an August fiesta into a September siesta. Cezanne and Picasso would have splashed Aegean blue and Provencal yellow on this English Riviera, where the daffodils bloom at Candlemas.

Mousehole lies in the parish of Paul, so-named because the church was dedicated to Pol de Leon, a Breton saint. The churchyard contains a memorial (1797) to Dolly Pentreath, claiming her as the last person who could speak Cornish. This memorial was erected by an amateur philologist, Prince Lucien Bonaparte, who seems to have been misinformed because Zennor churchyard contains a memorial to John Davey, claiming that he spoke Cornish in 1891, two centuries after Dolly Pentreath had died. Whence came the Cornish language? When did it perish? And why? Cornish is a form of Celtic speech. Chiefly because of Cornwall's remoteness, the language survived long after the rest of the kingdom had adopted a form of Saxon speech. In 1547 Andrew Boorde published *The Fyrste boke of the Introduction of Knowledge, the wych teache a man to speak parts of al maner of languages.* This encyclopaedia cited several examples of Cornish that bore some resemblance to Latin and French, as in *Pes myll eus a lemma de Londres?* (How many miles is it from here to London?) and *Gwrae, drewgh quart gwin de vi* (Hostess, bring me a quart of wine). The medieval Church had allowed Cornishfolk to use their own language when reading or reciting the Lord's Prayer, the Ten Commandments, and the Apostles' Creed. In 1549, however, the government announced that Cornwall must accept a wholly English Prayer Book. The reply was curt: 'we, the Cornish, whereof certain of us understand no English, do utterly refuse the new service'. In the end, of course, things temporal and commercial combined to anglicise the Celts. At the end of the sixteenth century William Camden reported that Cornish was dying: 'for the English speech do still encroach . . . and hath driven the same into the uttermost skirts of the shire'. Nevertheless, in 1640 the Vicar of Feock was still administering the Sacrament in Cornish. When an eighteenth-century philologist, Rev Robert Williams, failed to find two hundred subscribers for a projected Cornish dictionary, he expressed surprise because 'the Cornish gentry took so little interest in the language of their forefathers'. Twenty years later, Williams did publish his *Cornu-Brittanicum*, introducing it as 'the last attempt that was ever made to collect what remains of the ancient Cornish'.

Gaelic and Welsh have survived. Why, then, did Cornish die? There are two main reasons: first, Cornish has no literature that would justify the learning of a strange language; second, Cornwall is an English county, free from the anti-Englishry of Scotland and Wales. Quiller-Couch scorned the twentieth-century efforts to revive a dead language: 'I forsee,' he wrote, 'the terrible unreality which would infect the whole business . . . The only spectators properly impressed would be a handful of visitors and solemn antiquarians'. The tail of Q's prediction secreted a sting: 'If it has ever been your lot to witness the performance of a "literary" play in London and cast your eye over the audience it attracts, you too will know them and their stigmata . . . their ineffable attire, their strange hirsuteness . . .'.

In high summer there is no fitting approach to Land's End. All lanes thitherward teem with traffic. In September, by contrast, the lanes are relatively peaceful. In that peace I recollected some of the names which I had encountered en route: William Caxton, the Tenterden man, father of English printing; Thomas Gray, elegiac praiser of Buckinghamshire farmhands; King Edward of Islip in Oxfordshire; Oliver Cromwell of Huntingdonshire; Capability Brown and Algernon Swinburne of Northumberland; Wordsworth, the pinnacle of Lakeland; King Offa and his Marcher dyke; Mary Webb of Shropshire; John Masefield of Herefordshire; Coleridge in the Quantocks; Blackmore on Exmoor; Grenville at Bideford; Hawker in his Cornish parsonage. So much Englishry I had cited, and so much I had left unsaid, for who shall encompass a tapestry that is woven of prehistory, of Roman and Teutonic and Scandinavian history, of medievalism, of Tudor sea-dogs, Georgian inventors, Victorian industrialists, Atomic motorways?

Rounding a bend in the lane, I passed a group of harvesters toiling in the sun, proof that Cornwall did not rely wholly on cream teas and lucky charms. The flailing machines and the berry-brown men were modernity's reply to a report by the Board of Agriculture in 1794: 'The peninsular extremity of this island might be familiarly described as a rugged heap of rocks, rising abruptly out of the ocean . . . It may be said without risk, I think, that Cornwall comprises a greater proportion of *inarable lands*, than any other English county'. The same report mentioned an industry that has long since been outpriced by foreign competitors: 'The Mines of Cornwall consist chiefly of tin, copper, and some lead. The strata in which these metals are found, extend from the Land's End, in Cornwall, in a direction from west to east, a very considerable distance into Devon . . .'.

At four o'clock, with the sun as hot as ever, I stopped at the parish of Sennen, and there sipped tea in a field, less than three miles from the sea. Glancing through my notebook, I found a brief entry dated 1963: 'Sennen: 87 men went to the war from this tiny place. 11 of them never returned. 19 were related and had the same surname. While sitting on this coast, soon after the Battle of the Somme, Binyon composed his *dulce et decorum*:

They shall not grow old, as we that are left grow old:
Age shall not weary them, nor the years condemn.
At the going down of the sun, and in the morning,
We will remember them.'

I travelled the final mile of my journey on foot, and so came at last to Land's End, an alpha and an omega of England. Half a century ago Arthur Mee castigated the commercial squalor of the summer scene: 'Land's End by day is an abomination to all concerned, the messy home of litter louts'. Today the abomination has become even more abominable. In short, a good time is had by all save those who come to sample the solitude and to salute the sea. Yet the English could in one week erase the infamy be refusing to buy its wares. Fortunately, the peak of the profit motive had passed and with it, the hot dogs, ice creams, lucky charms, canned beer, and transistor cacophony.

Indeed, I counted only eleven people at Land's End, all of whom had come in the right spirit, for they either sat quietly or moved leisurely. Nevertheless, there are certain times and specific places at which even one stranger will seem as intrusive as a crowd.

Some people feel disappointed when they first see Land's End. The neighbouring cliffs at Pordenack Head, they say, are more impressive. Topography, however, has made Land's End a famous place, the most westerly in England, though several miles eastward of Ardnamurcham in Scotland. The scarred cliffs resemble the walls of a castle which the waves and the weather have besieged incessantly for thousands of years. Defoe offered a tribute that was both geological and teleological: 'Nature has thus fortify'd this part of the island of Britain in a strange manner . . . as if she knew the force and violence of the mighty ocean'. The ocean when I arrived was calm though never supine. Like a lion unaware of its playful strength, the rollers came lunging home with such power that, on meeting the rocks, they reared up and with a thunderous roar fell back, swamped by the next insurgent phalanx. The air vibrated with a steady thud while spray created a haze that was also a rainbow. James Smethem, the poet-painter, gave sound advice when he said: 'Always spell "Sea" with capital S, it is only right'. The prowess of English seamen was acknowledged by Chateaubriand, foreign minister to King Louis XVIII of France: 'If,' he wrote, 'you see the light of day on board *any* ship, provided it is under sail, you are *English born*; by virtue of the age-old customs of London, the waves are considered the *soil of England*'.

The sun was still hot, but in a few hours' time a watcher on this cliff would see the tiara of manmade stars glittering from the Longships light, the Lizard light, the Wold, the Bishop, the Pendean, and a constellation from the Scillies. Meanwhile, in two's and three's, the other visitors went away, leaving me to reflect that fashions will come and go, evanescent as the eddies on a stream; that mechanical gadgets will bring boons and banes beyond our power to imagine; that clothes, customs, laws, and languages will decay and die. But while men continue to live they will draw strength and comfort from the sun and the sea and the soil.

Suddenly a small boy appeared, evidently sent to retrieve a camera he left on the beach. Presently he gave a shout: 'Coo-ee! I've found it!' Then, by way of triumph, he picked up a smooth stone, and sent it skimming over the sea with seven sibilant splashes. What, I wondered, did the future hold for him and for a kingdom that had suffered Cardinal Wolsey's climacteric:

I have touched the highest point of all my greatness;
And from that full meridian of my glory
I haste now to my setting . . .

Princes and principalities may indeed founder swiftly, but genes are less easily disposed of. The nation that won at Crécy, and did not lose at Dunkirk; the nation that compiled Magna Carta, and devised Habeas Corpus, and patented steam engines; the nation that begat Chaucer, Spenser, Milton, Drake, Newton, Nelson, Lister, Constable, Dickens, Darwin, Elgar, Churchill . . . such a nation will experience some difficulty in destroying its inherited characteristics. It may become enslaved by an active minority, or debased by a listless majority, but it cannot undertake never to produce a second Shakespeare, a third Pitt, another Emily Brontë.

Turning from the Atlantic, I walked back to the car, my mission fulfilled, imperfectly yet with love; and while I walked, there came into my mind the words with which Michael Drayton saluted the rivers that

Down from these Western Sands into the sea do fall,
Where I this Canto end, as also therewithall
My England do conclude . . .

INDEX

Aisholt, 167
Alfriston, 35
Alnwick, 115
Alton, 71
Ambleside, 127, 131
Anmer, 81
Ascot, 28
Ascott, 49
Ashburnham, 18
Ashrigg, 26
Aston Cantle, 57

Bacton, 155
Barcheston, 51
Barton-on-the-Heath, 58
Barnstaple, 177
Bath, 92, 171
Battle, 19-22
Bellingham, 122
Bideford, 58
Billesley, 57
Birmingham, 55
Bishops Lydiard, 171
Bodmin, 182
Bonnington, 15
Boscastle, 180
Blakeney, 81
Bletchington, 48
Blickling, 81
Bradworthy, 177
Brailes, 55
Brampton, 66
Brancaster, 85
Branxton, 119
Bratton Fleming, 177

Cadbury, 181
Cadgwith, 183

Caldbeck, 138
Camborne, 182
Cambridge, 43, 67-73
Camelford, 181
Canons Ashby, 64
Canterbury, 13
Capel-y-ffyn, 154
Capheaton, 111-12
Charlecote, 58
Carlisle, 128-9
Charterhouse-on-Mendip, 166
Castle Acre, 76-9
Castle Cary, 171
Chatteris, 75
Chatton, 113
Chester, 145
Chipping Camden, 143
Chipping Norton, 49
Church Stretton, 146
Church Town, 149
Chysauster, 183
Clifton Hampden, 104
Cloutsham, 173
Clun, 147-8
Clyro, 154
Coates, 31
Cockermouth, 129
Coldstream, 119, 121
Combe Martin, 173
Corbridge, 108
Cornhill, 120
Cothelstone, 170-1
Coverack, 183
Craven Arms, 147
Crowcombe, 167
Cuckfield, 22
Cusop, 152, 154

Dorstone, 155
Dover, 11-13
Dulverton, 171, 173
Dungeness, 13-14
Dunmow, 42
Dunstable, 38

East Quantoxhead, 168
Ebchester, 101-2
Edale, 122
Ellesborough, 38
Elsdon, 113
Elworthy, 171, 173
Ely, 73, 75
Epworth, 92-3
Eton, 31-2
Ewelme, 38
Exeter, 173, 176

Fairy Cross, 178
Falmouth, 182, 183
Feock, 186
Ford, 118
Fotheringhay, 65
Fowey, 179
Frensham, 25
Fring, 82
Frome, 166

Glastonbury, 181
Glympton, 49
Grasmere, 127, 129, 138
Great Hampden, 38
Great Massingham, 79
Great Missenden, 39
Grosmont, 158
Gunwalloe, 183

Halford, 54
Hambleden, 38
Hampton-in-Arden, 58
Harbridge, 86
Hatfield, 94
Hawkshead, 134
Haxey, 94
Hay-on-Wye, 153-4
Haywards Heath, 22
Heathfield, 22
Helston, 181
Henley-on-Thames, 32, 35
High Halden, 15
Holford, 168-9
Holme-next-the-Sea, 76, 85, 89
Holt, 81
Honington, 50, 55
Horton-in-Ribblesdale, 122
Hunter's Inn, 173
Huntingdon, 65

Ickford, 41
Idlicote, 54
Ingleton, 122
Ingram, 115-16
Inkpen, 68
Islip, 48
Ipswich, 86
Ixworth, 76

Keighley, 95
Kendal, 99, 138
Keswick, 125, 129
Kettering, 65
Kineton, 57
King's Lynn, 73
Kington, 152
Kirk Yetholm, 122
Kirkby Lonsdale, 100, 138-9
Kirkharle, 103, 111
Kynance, 183

Lamberhurst, 149
Lanchester, 100
Landcross, 178
Land's End, 179, 186-7

Lechlade, 35
Leintwardine, 149
Lincoln, 90-2
Lingen, 150
Lingfield, 25
Little Langdale, 140
Littleport, 75
Little Walsingham, 82
Lizard Town, 183
Llandogo, 164
Llanthony, 154
Longwick, 41
Loweswater, 132
Luccumbe, 158
Lynmouth, 169

Macclesfield, 95
Maryland, 84
Matfen, 150
Marazion, 184
Maypole, 161
Meole Brace, 146
Merton, 177
Middleton-in-Teesdale, 100
Milton Street, 35
Minehead, 171
Monkton Combe, 65, 171
Monmouth, 163
Moreton-in-Marsh, 50-3
Morpeth, 120
Morwenstow, 179-80
Mullion, 183

Nether Stowey, 167
Newark, 92
Newstead, 98, 121
Northampton, 64
Norwich, 86

Otterburn, 112
Oundle, 65
Oxford, 42-7

Padstow, 41
Patterdale, 135
Paul, 185
Penrith, 129

Penzance, 184
Percuil, 182
Peterborough, 75
Peterchurch, 155
Pickering, 92
Piercebridge, 99
Plymouth, 176, 177
Polesworth, 56
Pontesbury, 146
Porthleven, 183
Potter Higham, 89
Presteigne, 150, 151-2
Preston, 42
Prestwood, 38
Priddy, 166

Raleigh's Cross, 172
Ravenspur, 96
Redruth, 182
Romney Marsh, 14-15
Rosedale Abbey, 92
Rothbury, 114

St Anthony-in-Rose-land, 182
St Austell, 182
St Bees, 131
St Enys, 185
St Gerrans, 182
St Juliot, 180
St Mawes, 182
St Michael's Mount, 184
Sandringham, 81-2
Sawrey, 134
Seathwaite, 132
Sedbergh, 65
Selby, 85
Sennen, 187
Shalford, 24
Sherborne, 78
Sheringham, 81
Shipley, 24
Shipston-on-Stour, 50-1
Shottery, 57
Shrewsbury, 146-7
Simonsbath, 174
Skenfrith, 161
Sleaford, 90

Slough, 36
Snitterfield, 58
Somerton, 171
Stanton-upon-Hine-
  Heath, 146
Stanton St John, 47
Staveley, 136
Stoke Poges, 36-7
Stratford-upon-Avon,
  53, 55, 58, 60
Sulgrave, 64
Swaffham, 76

Taunton, 171
Teddington, 31
Tenterden, 15-16
Thame, 41
Thetford, 86
Thockrington, 110
Tichborne, 42
Tintagel, 181
Tintern, 164-5

Tissington, 42
Titley, 152
Torquay, 176
Trelleck, 163, 164
Troutbeck, 127, 137
Truro, 182, 183, 184
Tynemouth, 120

Uckfield, 22
Ulpha, 133
Uppingham, 65

Veryan, 182
Vowchurch, 155

Warbstow, 181
Wareham, 38
Waterstock, 42
Watendalth, 138
Weedley, 82
Welcombe, 178
Wells, 171

Wem, 145
West Dereham, 79
Weston-super-Mare, 166
Whatcote, 54
Whatlington, 18, 19
Wheddon Cross, 174
Whitby, 96
Willington, 100
Wilmcote, 57
Winchester, 27
Windermere, 127, 135,
  136, 137
Windsor, 28-35
Wishford, 41
Woodchurch, 15
Wooler, 107, 115,
  117-18
Wythburn, 135

York, 89, 92, 94, 97-8

Zennor, 185